From Service To Success

ENDORSEMENTS

"Bob's book touched me at many levels. This is a must read for veterans, in particular combat veterans seeking to improve their personal lives. I quickly recognized that I am and have been on my own journey 'to Solitude' (Chapter 1) since serving in Desert Storm. Bob is bringing awareness to our nation's veteran suicide epidemic and providing practical solutions to help veterans and their families."

—Major General (retired) Mike Stone
Michigan Army National Guard

"Taylor writes with humility and authority, his passion for his fellow warriors is palpable and clear. From Service to Success *is difficult to put down."*

—Sandy Gallagher, Proctor Gallagher Institute CEO

"As a 10-year veteran from Special Operations, I can attest to the validity and importance of a book like "From Service to Success." *Bob's well-written and captivating book elicits an emotional response that creates a call to action for our Active Duty and Veteran members. His own military experiences gives him the ability to discuss how war can affect the minds of our men and women. An enticing and stimulating read for anyone that wants to improve themselves and conquer their own issues."*

—Former USAF Technical Sergeant Frank Troiano,
Pararescue Team Leader

"I served at Wilford Hall USAF Medical Center in San Antonio, TX and saw firsthand the challenges facing our active-duty members and their families, whether service or combat related. After my separation, my medical sales career affords me the privilege to work with DoD MTF's and VA hospitals in the eastern seaboard and so I continue to see the impact of service-related health and mental challenges faced by our active duty and veterans. From Service to Success *eloquently educates us on those critical issues and provides a simple road map for guidance and assistance ... An earnest effort by Bob to make a difference and a case for service—leadership."*

—Former USAF Sergeant Tony Bashir,
Ophthalmology Tech, Operation Room Tech,
and Honor Guard Wilford Hall Medical Center

"This book is a must read! It is inspiring, motivational and filled with humor through-out. Bob Taylor has done an exceptional job of taking you behind the scenes of his life and highlighting huge insights and principles that you can apply to any area of your life. He did an amazing job of bringing you along with him in his journey. Definitely recommended!"

—Jacquelyn MacKenzie,
Best Selling Author, International Speaker & Coach

From SERVICE *To* SUCCESS

New Mission, New Purpose, and a New Journey to a Great Life

BOB TAYLOR

NEW YORK

LONDON • NASHVILLE • MELBOURNE • VANCOUVER

From Service To Success

New Mission, New Purpose, and a New Journey to a Great Life

Published in New York, New York, by Morgan James Publishing. Morgan James is a trademark of Morgan James, LLC. www.MorganJamesPublishing.com

Proudly distributed by Ingram Publisher Services.

ISBN 9781636980171 paperback
ISBN 9781636980188 ebook
Library of Congress Control Number: 2022941942

Cover & Interior Design by:
Christopher Kirk
www.GFSstudio.com

DEDICATION

I dedicate this book to veterans. May it honor their service and sacrifices. To veterans who have lost their lives in service to their country, especially:

- Capt. Jon Olson, Radar Navigator
- Lt. Jorge Arteaga, Navigator
- Lt. Eric Hedeen, Electronic Warfare Officer

These men lost their lives in a B-52 incident near the island of Diego Garcia following a combat mission to Iraq during Desert Storm. To the many veterans who have sacrificed so much in duty and continue to endure the trauma of combat. To the far too many veterans who have lost their lives because of suicide from their post-combat struggles. To the veterans who contributed to this book (in order of appearance):

- Jeffrey Gramlich, my first interview, confirmed to me the importance of this book
- S.Sgt. Meg Krause, who was willing to share her deepest feelings in a very public way
- Maj. Jeff Hall, an officer who demonstrated how struggles impacted his whole family
- Lt. Gen. Harold Moore, a soldier's soldier and a leader's leader
- Marine Brian Escobedo, Army soldier Reagan, and Reagan's fiancée, who shared their personal stories
- Gordon Oosting, a Vietnam veteran who transitioned to civilian life in less than twenty-four hours after frontline combat

- Deshauna Barber, who exemplifies setting the highest of goals and perseverance

To the veterans in my family:

- My father, Carl Taylor, and father-in-law, Don Morey
- Brother-in-law, John Morey
- My uncles Red Henderson, Bob Scarlett, and Bill Scarlett
- My cousins Tom Henderson, Dean Morey, Wade Scarlett, and Doug Scarlett

To my B-52 crew during Desert Storm:

- Steve VanSciver, Aircraft Commander
- Bruce Way, Copilot
- Russ Barnes, Radar Navigator
- Ray Guidoni, Electronic Warfare Officer
- Ralph D'Avino, Tail Gunner

TABLE OF CONTENTS

Acknowlegments xi
Introduction: Desert Storm 1

Chapter 1: From Service to Solitude: 9
A Roadmap to Navigate the Difficult Transition to Civilian Life
Chapter 2: We're Always a Part of the Tribe: 25
Trading One Team for Another
Chapter 3: Building a Healthy Life After Service: 55
Forgiveness, Healing, and Recovery
Chapter 4: Creating Mental Stability: 81
The Science of a Healthy Mind
Chapter 5: Finding Physical Well-Being: .113
Adjusting to a New Type of Challenge
Chapter 6: Reconnecting with Support at Home: 139
Friends and Family Matter
Chapter 7: Finding a New Mission and New Purpose: 153
An Identity After Service
Chapter 8: Architecting a New Future: 169
Discovering Dreams, Wealth, and Aspirations
Chapter 9: From Service to Success: 193
Recognizing Key Strengths to Thrive

About the Author 217

ACKNOWLEDGMENTS

Writing a book was more difficult than I originally thought. It was a longer journey than I imagined; but it was worthwhile, and I learned so much. I sincerely believe that with all the help, we created a valuable book for readers.

The process: Justin Spizman is a bestselling author in his own right. He helped me create the structure of this book and organize my writings in a way that the reader can follow. He is a true book architect. *From Service to Success: New Mission, New Purpose and a New Journey to a Great Life* would not exist without Justin's editing and coaching. He always made me feel like I could do it, even when I didn't believe it myself. I am grateful for his wisdom and guidance. I also received the help from a good friend, Tina Longsteth. She very graciously offered to help me edit an early version of *From Service to Success.*

My support: My wife, Sara, who put up with "can you read this" more times than anyone could imagine. Even though she thought I was obsessed with my computer while I was writing, she had the patience and understanding I needed. She gave me the belief that I needed to finish the book. And, to my adult children, Jackie and Spencer; they inspire me to be better. Spencer has such a positive spirit, and that positivity is infectious. He has given me clarity when I've needed it most. I admire Jackie because of what she has accomplished through her personal drive and determination. Both have taught me that you can accomplish anything you can imagine. I have dedicated my life to making each of them proud, and I hope they see that.

My aspirations: Bob Proctor opened my mind to many more possibilities than anyone in my life before him. Spencer worked for Bob, and I received an invitation to one of his seminars. It lit a match inside my brain that started a fire of new thinking. I set goals that I wouldn't have considered before. Since that initial meeting, I have started two new businesses, bought a new $4.8 million building, purchased a lake house, founded a nonprofit organization for veterans, started glassblowing, and now have written a book. Bob Proctor passed away on Feb. 4, 2022. I'm disappointed I can't share this book with him because he was so instrumental in his encouragement for me to write it. I feel so honored to have spent one-on-one time with him and exchanged correspondence about things that were important to me. He was always incredibly gracious in his guidance.

Without Bob Proctor, I would not have met Jacquelyn McKenzie, who I consider to be a great friend. A push here, a nudge there, a listening ear, and the right words when I've needed them are her specialties. She has amazing intuition and has offered just what I've needed at the right times. Jacquelyn and Bob have helped me move further and faster, and I am so grateful for their support and friendship.

My adviser: Dr. Beth Dietzel is a hero to me. I am humbled by her dedication to helping veterans. She is amazing at what she does. I especially appreciate her efforts to get clearance from the Department of Veterans Affairs (VA) to answer some of my questions for this book. It is so helpful to get a professional's thoughts about the help veterans need.

My motivation: I asked Patti Knoles to help me design my book cover before I had even written a word. It helped me visualize a finished book and provided me with motivation throughout my writing. If I got stuck, I'd see the book cover and knew I had to finish it. I met Patti through a Bob Proctor event. I also met Peggy McColl at the same event. Peggy is a bestselling author multiple times over. She has such a wonderful smile and a subtle way of encouraging people to write books. I would have never considered the possibility of writing a book without Peggy convincing me that I could. Another Bob Proctor advocate, Doug Dane, also provided great motivation for overcoming my terror barrier, which I found too often; but I did overcome it.

INTRODUCTION:
Desert Storm

We're headed to "Cleveland."

The year 2021 marked the thirtieth anniversary of Operation Desert Storm. On January 4, 1991, I remember exactly where I was and what I was doing. I was on a tarmac at Griffiss Air Force Base in upstate New York. It was nighttime, and our deploying B-52 crews were getting ready to load up into a KC-135 to depart to our forward operating base, code-named "Cleveland." I remember seeing the bus carrying the wives and kids coming down the hill from our squadron to send us off. I have a picture of the moment with my wife, my two-year-old daughter, and me standing in a few inches of snow. My daughter was all bundled up in her snowsuit trying to stay warm while we shared our final minutes together as the crews waited to board.

I gave my wife and little Jackie hugs and smooches and turned when Lt. Col. Dean called us all to board. "It's time," he said. I turned and headed to the aircraft stairs. Lt. Col. Dean was our squadron commander, and he was standing at the top of the stairway, just outside the entrance to the plane. He was not happy to have to stay behind at Griffiss while his men headed into battle, but he was there to send us on our way. Our gear was already loaded, so all I carried up the stairs was the giant emotional lump in my throat from saying goodbye to my wife and daughter. I couldn't even talk when Lt. Col. Dean said goodbye. I just nodded and walked back to my seat. The people on that plane were very quiet as it took off for "Cleveland."

Operational security (OPSEC) dictated the nickname "Cleveland." I don't know who came up with it, but it stuck. Reporters were hounding the spouses to try to determine our destination. It was a secret, and we couldn't even tell our families. How could they answer a reporter if they didn't know themselves? They couldn't, and that was the point. B-52s were headed to Morón, Spain; Fairford, England; Jeddah, Saudi Arabia, and Diego Garcia. We didn't want the enemy to know how many were headed to which location, or even which locations.

"Cleveland" was in fact Diego Garcia, which is in the middle of the Indian Ocean near the equator, on the opposite side of Earth. To give an idea how remote the atoll is, it is described as 1,100 miles south of India, 2,197 miles east of Tanzania, and 2,935 miles west-northwest of Australia. Diego Garcia is near nothing. It is far from everything, especially from home.

So, we didn't tell our families where we were going, and we definitely didn't tell them what we were told during our specialized in-theater training out of Diego Garcia earlier in the fall. We were sent over for a month so we could fly over the Saudi peninsula in our rehearsal of upcoming combat missions if they were needed. Radar signals acted very differently over the desert sand, and they wanted us to witness this firsthand. In addition to flight training, we performed mission planning and attended briefings.

Two things stuck with me from my first trip to Diego Garcia. The first was a mission, a representative target for the first night or two of the war. We studied the terrain, the locations of defensive systems, and the targets. We planned it as though we were going to strike the target during combat. We presented our plans and strategies to the wing commander so he could be confident in our ability to handle the mission. The target was an airfield; the Iraqis had placed two surface-to-air missile systems at each end of the runway. The missile systems had look-down, shoot-down capability and they were placed on earthen berms to enhance their lethality. My entire crew wore glum expressions because we knew the B-52 could not evade these missile systems. Even though we knew that, those were our targets and we briefed it as though we would succeed. Had they been our targets on the first night, we would have surely been blown out of the sky. Fortunately, before the actual beginning of the war, those targets were reassigned to some European Tornado fighters. Tornados are supersonic fighters and held better chances against enemy defenses like those. Even still, the targets were so lethal that we lost several Tornados on the first night of the war.

The second thing I remembered from the earlier trip to Diego Garcia was a briefing we received from Gen. Horner, Commander of US CENTCOM Air Forces. We were part of the 4300th (pronounced forty-three hundredth) Provisional Bomb Wing, comprised of aircraft and crews from multiple B-52 air bases across the US. The 4300th Bomb Wing was the largest air wing ever assembled for combat operations. The auditorium was filled with the crews and support staff. At one point in his presentation, Gen. Horner turned to one of his staffers and asked loud enough for us to hear, "How many crew members are in a B-52?" I thought, *Holy crap, this guy doesn't know how many we have in a B-52.* Then he said, "Okay, it's six. So, we're expecting to lose forty-two of you guys. That's seven aircraft." I just remember thinking, *Well, thanks for the pep talk, General.*

So, when we left the tarmac that night in Griffiss, all of us had thoughts that we might not all be coming home. We really didn't have any idea how things were going to go.

As I said, Diego Garcia is a long way from anywhere. We were going there by way of several hellaciously long flights—eleven hours to Hawaii, nine hours to Guam, and then twenty hours to Diego Garcia. We were on schedule upon arrival into Hawaii, but the aircraft developed a problem that required a replacement part that wouldn't get there for several days. I felt guilty because our families were at home worried about us and there we were "stuck" in Hawaii. We did take advantage of some body surfing, snorkeling in Hanauma Bay, and a great Mongolian BBQ dinner at the Pearl Harbor Officers' Club. We eventually made it to the island, but four days late.

The war started for us several days later on the sixteenth of January (the first night of Operation Desert Storm), about twelve hours before anyone in the US heard about it. Roundtrip flights from Diego Garcia to Iraq were about nineteen hours long, not including the three to four hours of mission prep. My crew didn't fly a mission on the first night, but my aircraft commander came and gathered us so we could preflight a spare. We would get the systems of a spare B-52 all up and going, do all the preflight as though we would fly the mission ourselves, but just have it ready in case another crew needed it due to any issues with their aircraft. Everything was as usual until I entered the bomb bay. The weapons were different from anything I'd ever seen. The nav team was responsible for inspecting the weapons—and we didn't even have a checklist for these things. The guys from Munitions Maintenance Systems (MMS) came over and gave us a run-through.

There were wires hanging all over the place connected to each bomb. Apparently, just before weapons release over the target, a program would set timers for detonation every fifteen minutes. The target was an airfield. The purpose of the weapon was to bury itself deep underneath the penetrated runway, and then every fifteen minutes a bomb would explode. So, as personnel would start work on repairing their recently bombed runway, another bomb would explode fifteen minutes later—and another, and another. The thinking? Those randomly occurring explosions might deter someone from wanting to repair their runway. I'm pretty sure it was effective. Awesome idea, but who thinks of weapons like that? I wanted that job.

It was a good thing we figured it all out because as it was, a crew did need our aircraft and they were able to slide right in and take off on time.

I'll never forget that night. There were: thirteen B-52s rolling out one after another, twentysome air-refueling tankers, and several hot spares (aircraft launched and able to fly in case one dropped out). It is a sight not too many people have seen or probably will see again. The parade of planes taking off lasted for more than forty-five minutes as they flew into the darkness of the night. And, we still didn't know how it was going to go. How many would come back?

As it turned out, they all did that night. Not until a few weeks later did we lose three men in a B-52 accident as they were returning to the island after a combat mission. Lost were the radar navigator Capt. Jon Olson, navigator Lt. Jorge Arteaga, and electronic warfare officer Lt. Eric Hedeen. All of them were part of our cell (team). We had flown as a hot spare that night but returned to base after everyone was good to go. They were there the night before, and then they were gone.

A few weeks later, the ground war started. Then Chairman of the Joint Chiefs of Staff, Gen. Colin Powell, made it very clear what we were up to: "Our strategy to go after this army is very, very simple. First, we're going to cut it off, and then we're going to kill it."

As I write this book, I understand that other veterans have sacrificed far more than I have. At the same time, my experiences affected me and I struggled with nightmares, sleep deprivation, irritability, and relationship challenges. Combat affects us each differently. There is no one size fits all.

As I will point out several times in this book, my greatest regret is that I did not seek help much sooner. I waited for the same reasons most veterans delay, which we will discuss over the course of this book. I tried to fix things myself. I thought I had everything handled. Admitting that you have mental struggles can be embarrassing. So, I decided to write about that aspect of my life to point out that it's okay to share. You're not alone. A light shines at the end of the tunnel. Some amazing people have dedicated their lives to helping veterans.

More than anything, I want someone to read this book and find something inside of themselves that can become what they were truly meant to be. To reach their full potential. To find peace and happiness. To live how God intended for them. It is my most sincere hope that anyone struggling will find the help they need and realize the love and care many people have for them. To get the most out of *From Service to Success*, it might even be a good idea to read it with a friend, spouse, family member, or colleague.

This book contains: some of my military experiences, experiences as I struggled mentally, the work I did to overcome my adversities, other veterans' experiences both in their struggles and their success after the military, and some technical information to clearly explain what is happening to veterans' minds and bodies. If there is one theme to take away from this book it is the importance to communicate with others and always persevere. Remember, in the words of Winston Churchill: "Success is not final; failure is not fatal: it is the courage to continue that counts. Never, never, never give up."

Chapter 1

FROM SERVICE TO SOLITUDE:

A Roadmap to Navigate the Difficult Transition to Civilian Life

Ask most servicemen or women why they choose to serve our country, and often they will tell you the same thing: It is their calling. No other career may be more tasking and requiring of greater dedication and devotion. This is not an easy profession, but it is an extraordinarily respected one. We owe a tremendous amount of gratitude to those people who are willing to risk their lives, family, friends, and everything else they hold near and dear to ensure we continue to enjoy the freedoms afforded to us as citizens of the greatest country in the world.

The decision to enlist is often complicated, and each and every veteran has his or her own spin on the fundamental reasons why. But in the end, they all mostly feel it is a destiny of sorts ... a path they were always chosen to take. And for good reason. Our enlisted feel a tremendous amount of pride and satisfaction in serving their fellow citizens. Whether they do so domestically or overseas, there is no job like serving our country.

Why Do We Enlist?

The call to serve in the military has changed over the decades and has deep roots in complex social dynamics. Specific reasons are typically based on: the service of parents or relatives, a desire to prove oneself as a mature adult, financial needs, or pursuit of specialized skills. There is sometimes an assumption that money-related benefits and opportunities drive a person's decision to enlist, but most times that doesn't appear to be the case.

According to the Heritage Foundation, low-income families are significantly underrepresented in the military. US military enlistees disproportionately come from upper-middle-class families. Most in today's volunteer Army are not enlisting because they have no other economic opportunities but rather because they truly believe they can be difference-makers. Among other motivations, it is a calling from within, a deep-seated decision tied to their belief systems.

The bottom line: It is not always about the money and benefits, nor has it ever been. Though these perks sweeten the deal, they don't drive the decision. When they enlist, recruits are asked their top three reasons for joining the service. In seven of the past ten years, they have cited "patriotism" as one of those three motivators.[1] No surprise there. Those who argue that American soldiers risk their lives because they have no other opportunities belittle the personal sacrifices of those who serve out of love for their country. And most do. It is their calling, their purpose, and their identity.

---

1 https://www.heritage.org/defense/report/who-serves-the-us-military-the-demographics-enlisted-troops-and-officers

Actor Morgan Freeman was always entranced by war films, particularly pieces about fighter pilots. In love with the idea of flying, he joined the US Air Force in 1955 but was relegated to being a radar technician. His interest in flight was so strong that he opted to enlist instead of accepting a drama scholarship from Jackson State University.

From a personal perspective, I can share with you that my father greatly influenced my choice to join. He was an Army corporal and served in an ambulance unit in Germany during the Korean conflict. Listening to stories about him and my mom living overseas and the friendships they made inspired me to seek that same camaraderie. I even worked on a dairy farm for a summer, which was owned by one of his best friends from the Army. I strived for similar lifelong relationships. In addition, my uncle was an Army colonel. He was a Depression-era survivor who rose through the ranks based on his tremendous work ethic and dedication to his principles. I had great admiration for these two men, and I think it instilled in me a strong sense of duty to country. Their paths inspired mine.

After my dad passed away in 1982, I would often reflect on things he shared with me. One day while walking to my class at Michigan State University, I could clearly hear him saying to me, "I always wished I would have learned how to fly." In my case, I had always wanted to fly, and coincidentally, at the exact time I was hearing my dad's voice, I was walking past an Air Force recruiting station. I took the turn to the right and nine months later, I turned down an offer from General Motors to work as an engineer and instead I joined the Air Force's Officer Training School, making around $534 per month. As you can tell, it was definitely *not* about the money for me.

The tens of thousands of young men and women who have enlisted in the military in recent years grew up in the shadow of 9/11, often too young to remember the world prior to it. According to bestselling author Sebastian Junger, who wrote *The Tribe*, any simplistic understanding of "patriotism" does not begin to capture the myriad of motivations that often coexist alongside economic motives. As youth often put it, "I want to make a difference" is a major reason a significant number of people enlist.

When Junger asked soldiers in Afghanistan about their reasons for joining, they often said: "I joined the Army because of 9/11. We were attacked and we have to defend ourselves." Others fed on their family legacies: "My father fought in Vietnam; my grandfather was in D-Day … I don't wanna break that lineage of men in my family fighting." Some guys said, "Well, I sorta thought it might make a man out of me." All noble and easily respected reasons.

In a *Seattle Times* article by Tamara Rush nearly ten years following 9/11, Rush interviewed a twenty-year-old Marine recruit named Tim Freeman. Ten years earlier, Freeman was in fifth grade. His dad pulled him out of school after the first plane hit, and Freeman remembered being confused because all the grown-ups were either crying or stone-faced.

"It didn't really click in my head that it was a catastrophe," he said. A few days later, after his parents and teachers explained what had happened, Freeman made a promise to himself to join the military. As he grew older, he learned more about al-Qaida and terrorism, and his resolve to enlist grew stronger. "9/11 brought me closer to my country," said Freeman.

Some young men joined because they had relatives killed on 9/11 while working in the World Trade Center. In fact, this drove a thirteen-year-old who lost his uncle to the attack to decide he would be a Marine. He said, "It changed something inside of me. It made me want to fight for my country. We all became vulnerable. It became real."[2]

Surprisingly, military recruitment did not surge in the years after September 11; the Army met its recruitment goals in 2001 and 2002.[3] However, the Army missed its recruiting goal by over 7,000 recruits in 2005. In fact, the long-term recruiting landscape is not incredibly encouraging. But there is still great pride and a wonderful desire to serve our country. That will never change. Sure, enlistment numbers may rise and fall like any other profession, but the heart and soul of our servicemen and women will continue to shine through.

Many of these dedicated servicemen and women strongly identify with their time in the military. They find purpose, friendships, education, and some of the greatest life lessons you'd ever imagine as they navigate their enlisted lives. But eventually, that service either comes to an end or they are discharged to civilian life while awaiting another deployment or additional orders. Oftentimes during that gap, our veterans find themselves lost, unsure about how to navigate this dreamland at home. They no longer have a mission and awake each day to far different responsibilities.

In that context, America's 5,366 combat deaths and tens of thousands of wounded in Iraq and Afghanistan, have come as a terrible shock. Most young Americans associate the Army with coming home broken, physically, mentally, and emotionally.[4] In truth, many veterans transition easily back into their civilian lives. They have the support they need, a strong sense of purpose, and no real post-traumatic stress.

---

2 https://www.seattletimes.com/nation-world/9-11-inspired-many-young-americans-to-enlist-in-military/

3 https://www.seattletimes.com/nation-world/9-11-inspired-many-young-americans-to-enlist-in-military/

4 http://www.economist.com/news/united-states/21676778-failures-iraq-and-afghanistan-have-widened-gulf-between-most-americans-and-armed

But that story isn't true for every veteran. Some do indeed return to their families and friends as broken men and women, unable to transition back to life as they once knew it. They are depressed, unhappy, angry, and suffering from tremendous post-traumatic stress. In short, they are hanging by a thread and feel emotionally and physically trapped in this unfamiliar world at home.

These veterans are falling through the gaps, and we all have a collective responsibility to do something about it. It is easy to discuss the great pride and purpose servicemen and women enjoy while enlisted. But that conversation has got to continue once they arrive back home, feeling lost and unstable. Collectively, we all have a tremendous duty to serve those that serve us.

Veterans Are Falling Through the Gaps

The most astounding and troubling statistic anyone needs to know about veterans? On average, more than twenty-two commit suicide every day.[5] Over the last ten years, the number of suicides exceeded 60,000 men and women. That's more than were lost during the Vietnam War. An even more astounding statistic is that for every death by suicide nearly twenty-nine people *attempt* suicide but survive. Perhaps even more shocking, 250 people consider suicide.[6] This means that as many as 640 men and women who have served our military are attempting suicide daily and over 5,500 veterans think about suicide every day. That's jaw-dropping. Disappointingly, as many as 70 percent of those veterans receive no assistance through the VA. To say there is a gap that veterans are falling through is an understatement. There is a chasm. And it is growing.

---

5 http://www.militarytimes.com/story/veterans/2016/07/07/va-suicide-20-daily-research/86788332/

6 https://www.sprc.org/scope/attempts

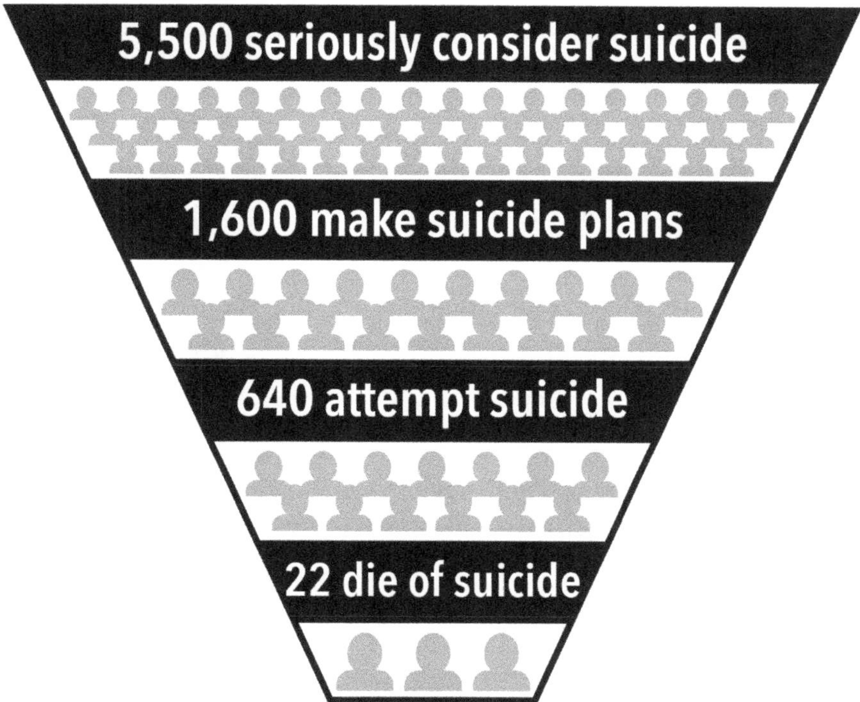

Of those veterans leaving military service, almost half have some level of PTSD symptoms. Only a portion of those realize they have any issues. A smaller group recognizes the need to seek help. An even smaller group seeks out help from the VA, and then only a very meager portion of them stick to those treatment plans. It's not all the fault of the VA. Some great people in the VA are working hard to bring exceptional mental healthcare to our veterans.

At times, veterans are their own worst enemy. Many younger vets do not see any value in proactively preparing for life outside the military. They enlist, serve, and figure they'll deal with the rest of it later.

Learning how the mind works is far from their priority when they are returning home. They believe they won't be affected by the challenges of transitioning. A cocktail of youth, machismo, infallibility, and just plain not understanding what is going on in their minds creates a situation where even if great help is available, many veterans either don't believe they need it or are too embarrassed to seek it; or they get too far behind the eight ball, falling into the traps of depression, substance abuse, and complete solitude. By then, it might just be too late.

The problem intensifies when veterans try to grapple with their own challenges while also trying to reassimilate into their family dynamic. Once they leave the military, husbands and wives, mothers and fathers, and sons and daughters find it difficult to adjust back into their relationships at home. They quickly discover that things aren't the same as when they left to go to war—and things are definitely different than the environment they just left during their duty. At the same time, sons and daughters, mothers and fathers, the entire family, and network of friends can't relate to what their loved one is experiencing. Then the disconnect occurs. The inability to reconnect to their "normal" relationships and handle the separation from their military teammates creates a sense of loneliness.

It Takes a Village

It literally takes a village to reacclimatize a service member to the norms of home. It is essential to recognize that family members, friends, loved ones, and colleagues all play a pivotal role in ensuring that this is a natural and normal transition. It may not always be easy, but we all benefit from a veteran securing a healthy lifestyle at home. This will help prevent these dedicated men and women from slipping through the cracks.

Together, we can create and bring to life a meaningful plan to ensure that they can turn it around and find a healthy and happy existence after experiencing the nightmares of war. They cannot do it alone. We can all provide a soft landing; we are part of their essential support system. As a mother, support your son. As a brother, support your brother. As an employer, find their strengths and utilize them in a positive manner. As a friend, be there and allow your friend to talk. It takes an army to fight a war, and it takes an army to support a soldier. Examples of this abound. One such example came to life while writing this chapter. My niece sent me a message while I was visiting Barcelona, Spain. She was unaware that I was writing this book. I am the only military person she knew, however, and she thought I could help.

Uncle Bob,

I have a very good friend who is suffering so, so badly from PTSD. He is up every night with his brain racing, suicidal thoughts. He recently confided in me he tried to hang himself. He ended up calling his mom and dad over to be with him and talk. My husband has been staying up with him until around 9p then he goes home and is alone. I want to help him and help us too. Are there any resources you could share?

He is currently being treated at two VA facilities. He says the medicine makes him feel so numb and out of body so he stops taking it. Then he starts self-medicating for a month. REPEAT. One of these times his rollercoaster is going to derail. I am really scared for him.

His story: He was in the Marines and did tours in Afghanistan. The last one was very bad. There was an attack. Most of his "brothers" did not come home. He has a scar covering his body. He does not talk about the events much. When he does it makes me so sad and helpless. Obviously, he isn't getting what he needs from the VA to cope with daily life.

Any resources would be greatly appreciated.

Sadly, this isn't the first email I've received like this. Even worse, there really are no easy answers. My niece and her husband are doing all they can without knowing about the available resources. I'm sure that this former Marine was seeking help, and his support system is connecting in a way that gives him hope to go on another day. This story feels very personal to me. I don't want anything to happen to this young man, and I recognize he is one of the many. It becomes obvious that this is not just a veteran problem. It's also a problem for everyone with close relationships with these veterans, including my niece and her husband.

Though these veterans feel alone, the hard truth is that they are not. They are more like their fellow veterans who are suffering in similar ways, and they don't even realize it. By being alone, they are missing the camaraderie that held them together and brought them home safely. The same group capable of achieving unbelievable things in combat is the one that could possibly come together and work to overcome the biggest challenge of their lives: transitioning home and developing a completely new mission and new purpose.

Often, it takes more than the veterans themselves and their ill-equipped family and friends to remedy the situation. It will take a combined effort of professional counseling, better access to help for friends and families of veterans, and a new approach to helping each and every veteran with a softer landing when coming home.

In the end, the VA is only seeing a very small percentage of veterans in need. Sadly, some of those veterans are not even following the treatments prescribed. We are leaving a large swath of veterans without the care they need, no coping skills, no way to know how to deal with their problems, and an entire network of families, friends, and people who care about them with absolutely no way to know how to help.

Regardless of one's views about the VA's ability to care for veterans and what we may believe about the right and wrong way of caring for them, we can no longer sit back, watch this happen, and point the finger of blame at anybody else. As a group, we must act immediately to understand what is happening and why so many veterans are slipping through the gaping gaps in our system of care.

One Falls, We All Fail

When even one soldier falls, we all fail. Since we are in this together as a collective country, we all have an important responsibility to help those who have served our country adjust back to life as civilians. But when even one soldier succumbs to suicide, depression, drugs, alcohol, or even worse, we have all failed as a society. If we are willing to enjoy that which they fight for, we should also share in ensuring their happiness and success when/if they return home.

Whether we realize this, **we are all in this together**! No one is untouched by the tragedies of the returning vets who take their own lives or fail to acclimate to their new lives at home. Millions of people are out there like my niece, having to constantly worry about her friend. The relationships take a toll on everyone involved. Moms and dads don't understand why their son with so many decorations and medals could possibly be depressed, especially when they are so proud of him. The veteran gets frustrated because no one understands her. The friends feel like they can't connect in a way that is meaningful. Then the worst occurs.

Employers are missing out on hiring great talent because they can't understand the connection between the values, discipline, and drive necessary to be great in the military. These qualities could be a tremendous asset to their companies. Getting jobs is not the answer alone. The ultimate goal is to help veterans find their passion and support them in living out their dreams. Employers can play a role in that by doing more than just interviewing. They can also work to understand the deeper aspects of these veterans as individuals. While veterans may not be good at translating their military skills into civilian strengths, employers can learn how to help translate that for them. It's a worthwhile investment. Specialized training programs within companies can help veterans just like any other personal development program can.

The encouraging part is that a great deal of help exists out there. However, the dots aren't being connected between veterans and the help they need. That's the gap this book will help bridge.

As a society, we need to educate ourselves and encourage veterans to find the right help at the right time. Families need to be equipped with the ability to identify problems and guide their family members to seek and follow treatments for their PTSD symptoms. The chief aim of this book is to provide some of that information and at least a glimmer of hope to struggling vets.

In Their Own Words

Jeffrey Gramlich served as a sergeant in the United States Marine Corps. He was stationed out of Camp Lejeune, North Carolina, in the infantry, motorman specialist. He did a tour in Afghanistan in 2004 and a tour in Iraq from 2005 to early 2006, about fourteen months total with deployments. Jeffrey shared his story with me and opened up to provide a glimpse into his experiences during his transition from military service. When asked about his return home, he said:

When you get out of such serious circumstances and all that, basically when you come back you're at a loss in the transitional phase as to what benefits you're able to obtain from your active duty. They gave you a small brief, but not much, so you were left to go down to the federal building and figure it all out. Not to mention on top of that, barriers to employment. For example, an infantry guy who has two tours in Iraq, that was basically kicking down doors and all that kind of stuff, how does that relate to the civilian world? That was really hard to explain to employers. You had a lot of leadership. You had a lot of discipline. You had a lot of specialties, accountability with weapons systems and just handling millions of dollars' worth of equipment and being accountable for a team of people. That didn't make sense to many employers, so you would be overlooked for job interviews or you couldn't really put it into words on a résumé. There was a huge gap between civilians and military veterans. You can sense that right away because they wouldn't have an idea of what you were talking about or where you were coming from.

In his struggles beyond finding a job, Jeffrey shared some very personal aspects of his return:

I personally went through PTSD diagnosis and just trying to figure out what's wrong with me and it's not like something's wrong with you, it's just the result of combat trauma and whatnot. Trying to mesh into the civilian world, basically dealing with anger and bitterness and resentment and survivor guilt. All those kinds of things that you were basically learning to digest and I mean, I got out ten years ago almost and I'm still, I just got a counseling session this morning at eight a.m. I'm still digesting through a lot of it. Just to realize that it's an ongoing personal process to readjust, it's not an overnight thing. For me, if I didn't go through it and acknowledge that something was up, I don't know where I would be.

.... The one thing I would like to change is, I probably would've listened sooner than later. Pretty soon after I got out, they were telling me drinking is not the answer. You might want to seek out help from the VA. My pride was saying, no, no I'm good. I'm good, I'm good. I probably would've come to sobriety sooner and started to go towards the counseling a little heavier. I'm not saying that it's taking up a lot of my time now, but I would be a lot further than I am today.

.... What I'm most proud of? I would say that I've been able to accomplish a lot. I got up to my graduate degree with my GI Bill. I'm now employed full-time at a veterans' one-stop center in Buffalo. We do all things vets, financial counseling, all sorts of things where we lead the vet in the right direction, so I guess I'm proud that I was able to turn my seeming demons or what was supposed to take me down into strengths and positives and make a difference and be an influence within the veterans' community, I swear because this carries into other things too as well.

I think for every human being, having a sense of purpose is obviously in our DNA. Especially after the military, I think it's critical, readjusting vets, redefine and refine that sense of purpose because you had such a purpose when you were in the military to wake up each and every day. When you lose that, you feel a loss of identity and a loss of man, what's next? To be honest, I was in infantry, so there's a lot of adrenaline to it, you know?

Then, when you come out, trying to find that purpose, it seems like a lot of things are mundane or boring, just to be an accountant or work in the civilian world. Really, trying to find that purpose is so critical because it's going to make the difference in your readjustment. Redefining it is definitely, not easy but you got to step in the directions that make sense to you.

Jeffrey is just one example of the magnitude of the problem. He might be one of the lucky ones because he can now open up and fundamentally share how he feels. Many vets remain trapped in their own minds, unable to fully comprehend exactly what is going on. It is important for each of us to fully comprehend the extensive damage we've undergone by serving our country. More importantly, we, as human beings, must come together and work to support those we love so that they can transition back to life as civilians. We will have to overcome bumps in the road and obstacles, but we all have a collective responsibility to be part of the solution.

Those who are willing to sacrifice all to fight for our freedom are extremely special. They protect us at home and overseas. They search to spread hope to underserved nations and protect those who cannot protect themselves. But when they return home, they need that same protection. Each of us must invest in the lives of those who serve us. Our support is paramount.

This is a journey we will share together.

Chapter 2

WE'RE ALWAYS A PART OF THE TRIBE:

Trading One Team for Another

People often say that servicemembers are the largest alumni group in the world. Quite possibly that is true. The United States Armed Forces consist of the Army, Navy, Marine Corps, Air Force, Coast Guard, and now the new Space Force. For 2020 alone, we recognized and celebrated almost 1.3 million men and women who were faithfully serving our country. We support them with a budget of over $989 billion. In short, we are very serious about our armed forces and those that fight for each of us. The United States military dates back to 1775, and in just the first eight years, over 217,000 men fought for our country. That number has grown year over year, and today we can likely recognize tens of millions of honorable men and women who enlisted.

Tribe for Life[7]

The military is a tribe we join just once but remain a part of for the rest of our lives. You can span the world and likely find an alumnus in almost every corner. That is in part because America has more than 800 foreign bases and a presence in many foreign countries. This is a tribe without boundaries or limitations. Serve once, be a cardholding member forever. But the sheer size is just part of it. The armed forces offer members a remarkable level of camaraderie, friendship, mentorship, and relationships. Some days you feel like you are in college, and other days you feel like you've graduated to the most challenging and difficult experiences imaginable. But through it all is a close-knit group of other officers and enlisted men and women, by your side, experiencing the good times and the bad with you.

The internal workings and connections within the military are extremely unique. Likely, you cannot fully comprehend it unless you have spent time in the "trenches." That is not to say that you cannot understand it, but it is a special experience understood best by those involved in it. You see, military people treat military people differently than they do anyone else. When deployed, they are with the same folks day after day. We spend more time with these people than with our own families, which is sometimes sad but also necessary to build the trust we need to run into battle and protect one another. But so much occurs before we even march onto that battlefield.

Humor, extreme sarcasm, and a healthy dose of stupid pranks and teasing are the mainstay of military camaraderie. We have to do something to pass the time. We used to say, "Got a scab, we'll pick it." Nobody's safe from the banter; it's part of the fabric of deployments. That's what happens during the monumental amount of time during

---

7 http://www.realwarriors.net/multimedia/profiles/reintegration.php

training, the extended times of hurry up and wait, or the dwelling time between combat operations. The twenty-four seven time spent with people with a lot of time on their hands creates some funny and not-so-funny memories, but it is a common bond for anyone spending any time in the military.

In addition, servicemen and women experience an immense sense of family or camaraderie while deployed. Reliance on others for their own survival and their commitment to the lives of everyone around them is a completely different level of relationship than what they had before they left. This isn't your typical work relationship. These bonds intensify because the military 'family' has experienced some of the most extreme forms of stress and even grief together. Those types of relationships do not exist when they return home. It all just seems to be much more superficial. The connections and the common goals are just not as intense.

Being part of something larger than themselves, the enormous sense of team, the massive shots of adrenaline from being in combat, the sense of purpose, and always being a part of some mission or common goal are just a few of the reasons veterans relate to one another more than anyone else. Joseph Kearns Goodwin, a former captain in the US Army,[8] shared:

> The returning soldier is no longer part of a group bound together by a clear sense of purpose, familiar rituals, and shared experiences. Relationships forged under fire cannot be easily recreated in the modern world or even understood by anyone who has not been in combat. This is especially pronounced in the modern era of warfare, when such a tiny percentage of the population is actively engaged in America's conflicts. Yet, if we are to reach our troubled soldiers, we

8 http://niemanreports.org/articles/bonds-of-friendship-on-an-emotional-journey/

must begin to understand that feelings of isolation and the absence of camaraderie combined with the loss of clear purpose weigh as heavily as the memories of the bodies, bombs and bullets.

Here is a story I relay to highlight the intense experiences shared during combat. Not until six months after I returned home did I start having vivid and violent nightmares—a parting gift from these intense experiences, along with the other ten combat missions we flew and the stresses associated with combat. Hopefully, you can see in this story the closeness and trust required to be successful in our missions. These intense emotional connections and shared experiences are difficult to recreate and can lead to the lifelong challenges many of our veterans face:

War Story: First Combat Mission

(January 19, 1991: Third night of Desert Storm in a low-altitude B-52 strike)

To avoid air defenses, B-52s flew at low altitude (200 feet or so above the ground) for the first three nights of the war. This was the first war where B-52s flew in combat at low altitude. Even so, we had trained for years to do this. All my training and the crew's practice missions had prepared us for this. Was I nervous? Yes. Under stress? Yes. Even with that, we were absolutely ready.

My crew was from Griffiss AFB, but we were stationed at Diego Garcia BIOT (British Indian Ocean Territory), a naval base 700 miles off the coast of Madagascar. Just know that it's a very long way away from home.

"Luxor Flight, check. Two, Three." It was the radio check for Luxor Flight, a cell of three B-52s ready for takeoff. I was the navigator (Nav) in Luxor Two.

"Luxor Flight, power up." The lead aircraft was starting their takeoff.

"Pilot-Nav, timing." Every communication on the interphone was short, to the point, and always led with who you were talking to, followed by who was talking. I notified the pilot that I was keeping track of the time so we could take off precisely one minute later. Two nights earlier, I had watched my buddies take off with the same spacing. One by one, all the refueling tankers and bombers took off for approximately forty-five minutes straight in one-minute intervals. I'd never seen anything like it, and no one knew how many would be coming back the next day. Now it was our turn.

"Pilot-Nav, coming up on one minute. Ready, ready, now."

"Luxor Two, power up." Our aircraft commander announced our official roll.

"Nav-Pilot, S-1 now." We were rolling along at approximately 480,000 pounds loaded with 50,000 pounds of bombs and a whole bunch of fuel. S-1 was the first aircraft speed we reached to help the pilots determine if we could take off.

"Pilot Nav, timing."

"Pilot-Nav, coming up on 13.8 seconds, ready, ready, now."

"Crew-Pilot, S2, we're committed." We had reached a speed where we would no longer abort if something went wrong. We would take any problems into the air.

This was the beginning of my first combat mission; but actually, the mission had started almost five hours earlier. The commander of the unit had briefed us. Then, he introduced the targeteer. This guy was the evil genius on the base. He chose the weapons we would use, the number of B-52s to strike the target, and whether we would attack the target on a single axis or multiple axes. Tonight, we were taking 50 Mk 117 (pronounced Mark one-seventeen) Snake-eyes bombs for each of the three B-52s to prevent our enemy from supplying their war assets.

After the briefings, we would study the mission, the charts, the targets, the comm plan. We would talk about potential emergency procedures and crew coordination stuff. It was something we'd done hundreds of times in training. This had a different feel to it—more focus, less humor. Four years of training had led me here. We continued our climb-out and departure.

"Pilot-Co, we've got an overtemp on number seven." The seventh of eight engines had reached a temperature that got the attention of the copilot. The two pilots went through their checklist.

"Pilot-Crew, we're going to shut number seven down. Nav, dig in and see what our mission go/no-go says." Almost every contingency was spelled out. If we decided we were a no-go, we still had what was called a hot spare crew in the flight cell. It was an extra B-52 that had done all the same prep that we did; it was airborne with us in case one had to turn around. We needed to know if we should continue or have the hot spare return to base.

"Pilot-Nav, we're still go."

That put a lot on the pilots' shoulders. Without the seventh engine, the aircraft wouldn't climb and maintain altitude the same. We would need to use a special technique called tobogganing for air-refueling. They would get to the right altitude, connect with the KC-135, but then both aircraft would gradually descend while refueling to stay connected. This would have to be repeated many times that night. It took great skill.

While all this was going on, one of our three navigational computers shut down. If we lost another one, we would be without our fully automated bombing system and our accuracy would have been severely degraded. This had happened several years earlier on a training mission, and the outcome was not good (but that's another story). The radar navigator (Radar) and I shut down the whole system and rebooted over the Indian Ocean using our newly installed GPS system to help bring us back online. We would rather shut things down over the ocean than have the system fail at a more critical time, like over the target. Normally, we would have told the crew what was happening, but Radar and I decided to go ahead and deal with our problem and let the pilots deal with theirs.

It took two and a half hours to reboot, and it came up just as we were approaching the Arabian Peninsula. The pilots handled two air-refuelings incredibly well. Our systems were almost fully up to speed. Time to run our inflight terrain avoidance (TA) checklist to prepare to fly at low altitude. We were starting our descent into low altitude, dropping from 28,000 feet to about 5,000 feet on our way to our eventual altitude of 200 feet above the ground. We had been following Luxor Lead without any radio communication. We could see them in spite of the dark of night using our infrared (FLIR) system and the night vision (STV). We could see through the two monitors, which were our only "windows" to the outside world in our downstairs "office."

I read aloud a warning on the chart when we crossed into Iraqi airspace. It cautioned that we could be shot down. It got a chuckle from the crew. We had descended now into low altitude, hyperfocused. As the nav, I was constantly plotting our position and keeping the pilots aware of terrain height. Radar was heads down in the radar screen and watching for terrain that we were below. One pilot was on night-vision goggles (NVGs) and the other was flying instruments. The copilot, "Co," was eyes out on NVGs looking at the terrain.

"Pilot-Radar, terrain three miles—above us, advantage right." That meant that we were flying below terrain in front of us. We would either need to climb over it, fly to the right, or fly to the left of it.

"We're moving right," the pilot responded.

I was watching the radar altimeter that responded with our height above the ground. It was running around 150 to 250 feet. The B-52's wingspan is 185 feet, so we were low.

"Crew-EW (pronounced 'Crew E-Dub'), I'm picking up a fighter, searching eleven o'clock." The EW could see the radar signal of an enemy fighter at some distance about eleven o'clock off the nose of the aircraft. "It's off a ways." He was not certain of distance, just that the signal wasn't as strong as an aircraft close by. In training, the EW would make these announcements from simulated signals and everyone knew there was no threat. Tonight, it was real. So, for real, a fighter out there somewhere was looking for someone just like us.

"Searching," the pilots acknowledged; they were looking for a fighter, but we never heard or saw anything.

"Pilot-Radar, terrain on the right ahead, stay left."

"Radar-Co, I've got it visually." Co could see the feature in his NVGs. The pilot kept the aircraft flying along with a terrain avoidance (TA) line on the screen, set at 200 feet. The Iraqi terrain is not a flat desert like the Arabian Peninsula. It's rocky and hilly, which made it great terrain for our low altitude tactics.

"Staying left-Radar."

"Crew-Nav, let's run the Before IP Checklist." We needed to brief the bomb run, get everyone prepped for the target, and preset some of our bombing systems. After the short briefing, there was the checklist.

"Pilot-Nav, target area altimeter is two-niner-eight-niner." We had to make sure the altimeters were set correctly so our altitude would be correct. Kind of important when you're that close to the ground.

"Two-niner-eight-niner, set-Nav." Every other part of the checklist was run silently with hand signals. The noise inside made verbal communication impossible—even with the person you're sitting next to.

The bomb run would last about ninety seconds, but we had to make a big 120-degree turn to the right. We had to do everything right, so we would roll out at full speed and on time (plus or minus ten seconds). If we were ten seconds early, we would fly into the fragments (frag) of the lead aircraft's bombs. If we were ten seconds late and dropped our bombs, we would frag number Three. At about one minute before the turn, I would give the pilots a heads-up.

"Pilot-Nav, this will be a right turn to zero-seven-five degrees."

"Got it, Nav."

"Pilot-Nav, come right zero-seven-five, use fifteen degrees of bank." The bank angle would dictate how wide or narrow the aircraft would turn. Fifteen degrees was the standard.

"Roger, Nav."

Thirty seconds later: "Pilot, give me eighteen degrees." I could tell we were rolling a little wide. We needed a steeper angle to turn tighter. "Give me three-two-five on your airspeed."

"Roger, Nav, how we lookin'?"

We rolled out four seconds late. I'd forgotten about the number seven engine being down, so we couldn't quite get the speed I wanted. "Shit," I said under my breath. I wanted to nail it exactly on time, but we were within our ten seconds.

The radar and I ran our bomb run checklist. Normally, that took about fifteen seconds, but this time it only took about three. It went so fast, we looked at each other and decided to run it again to make sure we did it right. We had. That's the thing about hyperfocus and adrenaline. Time seemed to slow. Our training was so ingrained, it was like muscle memory.

"Eighty-five TG Crew. We're running four seconds late. We're good to drop." That meant we had eighty-five seconds to go. We were at maximum airspeed for the run and could safely drop our weapons. Radar and the pilots kept calling out terrain, and I had a second to look out front in the STV (night vision). I could see sparkly things on the screen. It looked like the sparkles that fell from fireworks. I'd never seen that before. I wondered what it was, and then it struck me. "Oh yeah, they're shooting at us." It was the first time I'd seen it, and it took a hot second to realize what it was. Wait!? It was even before the lead aircraft was at the target. They were already shooting. So much for sneaking up on 'em.

I prayed. I bowed my head and asked God to guide the pilots. My two fists rested on the tabletop in front of me for emphasis. Mk 117 Snake-eyes were 1,000-pound bombs with metal fins that would snap open after exiting the aircraft. The air resistance from the fins would pull the bombs back behind us so they wouldn't blow up right underneath us. We couldn't drop at 200 feet above the ground though. We were supposed to release at 400 feet.

"Crew-Pilot, I've got a cloud deck at 600 feet. I'm going to climb into that for the release to keep out of visual."

So, he did. Normally, flying higher over a target was more dangerous, but when the enemy is shooting antiaircraft guns at you, not letting them see you is a good thing. Smart pilot.

"Ten seconds, Crew. Five, four, doors open, one—bombs away."

I counted it down. Our FLIR and STV monitors followed the point where Radar had put his crosshairs. Yep, it was the target. I looked over and watched the Bomb Release Interval Computer (BRIC) lights tick off as each bomb fell away. The BRIC determined the time between each release so that the 50,000 pounds would fall in the desired target train.

Two lights stayed on. A quick double-check and we reset the BRIC, but the lights stayed on. The pilot's release light was on too, so he already knew what was coming.

"Crew-Radar, we've got two hung." Two of the 1,000-pound bombs were still attached to the aircraft. Carrying them back with us was not an option. We didn't know what configuration they were in. That meant they could be armed and ready to blow up.

"Roger, Radar, my light's on too," said the pilot.

We went to the emergency release checklist, which was authorized for combat missions only.

"Bombay doors open, Pilot." Radar then configured the release and initiated the releases with the master bomb switch.

"Bombs away, Crew," I announced. We just dropped a couple of 1,000-pound duds.

We were still post bomb run and still running checklists. Luxor Three had just finished flying over the target behind us.

"Crew-Co, we're coming up on a radio frequency change." At certain times, we had to change frequencies to confuse the enemy or make it harder for them to listen in. Co made the change.

"Luxor Flight, check?" Lead Pilot called for a check.

"Two." A few seconds passed, but Three did not check in.

"Luxor Flight, check?" "Two" … Time passed, but again, no Three.

"Luxor Flight, check?" "Two." Still no Three. Talk of search and recovery was brought up. Eight or nine minutes passed.

"Luxor Flight, this is Three. Sorry, we were late on the radio change." We'd have to talk about that one when we got back. We really thought he got it. It wouldn't have surprised me by the amount of AAA (antiaircraft artillery). Our copilot later told us that he saw yellow and orange tracers coming up through the clouds, indicating they were shooting

80mm to 120mm rounds of lead at us. That's three-inch to almost five-inch rounds. I'm pretty sure my Kevlar vest wasn't going to help.

We started our climb-out.

"Pilot-Guns, I've got a bogey at four o'clock six miles." The gunner in a B-52 sat in the crew compartment next to the EW. He could see a fighter on his radar screen.

"Roger, Guns."

"Looks like he's closing." The gunner could see the blip on his radar getting closer. I distinctly remember thinking, *Doesn't this stop?* It seemed like one thing after another.

"Roger, Guns." The pilot then called for AWACS support. He asked in code if he could see a bogey behind us.

"Negative, Luxor."

"Pilot-Guns, he's coming to six o'clock and four miles. Do you want me to shoot?" I was like, "Hell yes. Shoot him."

"Hold on, Guns." He called AWACS again.

"Negative."

"Pilot-Guns, he's still closing, three miles. Should I shoot?" *Holy shit,* I thought. *He can just as easily blow us out of the sky*. It was maximum pucker factor.

"Hold on, Guns." Another call to AWACS.

"Negative, Luxor"

"Are you sure, 'cause we've got a bogey on us and we're getting ready to shoot him."

"Uh, Luxor, that's not a bogey, that's an F-16 giving you an escort." I thought it would have been mighty helpful if he had told us that on the first check. Maybe we should make a change to the code words to just ask, "Is there a fighter behind us that we need to shoot at, or is it a friendly?"

"Tell him that's not a good place to be tonight." Fighters should never get behind a B-52 after a bomb run. I guess he didn't know about the four barrels of machine guns aimed at him. After the brief warning from AWACS, he turned and went home.

Still on our climb-out, and Lead told us he was experiencing some shudder and control issues. He asked us to come closer to look at his tail for possible rudder damage. When we got closer, our FLIR camera showed us that a portion of the aircraft aft of the rudder was damaged and jagged and the chute was deployed. B-52s use the chute for landing to help stop the big aircraft on the runway. The tail of the aircraft had been shot off over the target. After a few minutes, Lead made a call.

"Two, you take the lead. We're going to Jeddah for an emergency landing."

"Roger, Two has the lead. Good luck."

Another air-refueling, our third for the night, eight more hours, and we landed. That was definitely enough for one night. I also knew I had a great crew. A great crew!

The memories always stay with us. Each experience, each mission, and of course, each and every loss. And as they say, you never forget your first time. The relationships forged in the crucible of combat are nearly impossible to compare to those formed in a civilian workplace. We, as veterans, need to know and understand that. We also must find ways to do the best we can to connect in whatever way we can. It is not easy. And no, no one can really understand our wartime experiences. At the same time, we must build anew the tribes with which we will spend the rest of our lives.

The Tribe Is Around You

Before entering the military, each person was a member of one or more tribes. It could have been their family, a group of friends, a sports team, and possibly a volunteer group. It is impossible to go through life and not be a part of some tribe. Every human being seeks to be loved and to belong.

Psychological science explains the bonding that occurs within the military. When people enter it, or are on deployments, they become part of a new tribe and have a need to belong to it. According to Maslow's hierarchy of needs, basic emotional needs drive their sense of needing to belong. The need for love and belonging are only behind the basic physiological needs (food, water, and shelter) and safety needs (personal security, financial security, health, and well-being).

Some species live largely alone, while others, such as *Homo sapiens*, have learned that forming a tribe allows us to share work and live a safer life. As for the military tribe, each member has gone through a predictable sequence of: acknowledgment (being recognized), approval (being sized up), and then acceptance before being admitted into the tribe. To each person, the process is about gaining respect, building self-esteem, and gaining status, all of which are tantamount to fitting in.

It's not surprising that, once a veteran leaves the military, they do so with these intense bonds and a strong sense of tribal belonging. Remember, they've just left their most trusted tribe and feel a sense of loss. After sixteen years of being a civilian, I still tell people I miss the camaraderie of my time in the military. Nothing is comparable in the civilian world.

Even though a significant number of veterans transition back into known tribes like family and friends (and even new tribes, like the civilian workforce) relatively seamlessly, more than one in two veterans do not. Without actively working at it, many veterans are unskilled and unprepared to find a new tribe—or to even reconnect with their previous ones. The tribe is out there, but roadblocks exist to finding it. The inability for a family to fully understand the shared experiences of being deployed creates the "they don't get it" mentality on behalf of the veteran. It's also frustrating for the family who just cannot understand how their tribe member feels.

Upon their return from service, many veterans feel alienated from their families and communities. The only ones who "get them" are their old service buddies, and they're no longer around. The bond that is built through shared hardship isn't present when no hardship exists. This leads to a level of disconnectedness and feelings of loneliness.

Many veterans view themselves as alone in their struggles, often believing that their fellow veterans are coping just fine. This can then lead to a strong sense of isolation. Unprepared for these new feelings of anger, shame, depression, and confusion, the veteran resigns himself or herself to dealing with things on his or her own. In fact, many reject their family's attempts to help and just want everyone to leave them alone. *They fear the anger they struggle to control.*

Without knowing it, these isolated and disconnected veterans are already part of a tribe, a community filled with veterans with similar experiences. These tribe members probably understand how it feels to be lost, unable to sleep, have nightmares, and turn to alcohol or substance abuse; they understand the whole host of additional challenges veterans face. In fact, many of those veterans are actively looking for veterans they can help. The VA is in search of struggling veterans to help, and more veteran service organizations than we can count exist. The very tribe that kept people going through some of the most difficult periods of their service is still available—just in a different form.

Furthermore, while the families and friends don't "get them," they still care and want to learn how to better understand how to help. The ingredients are all there waiting to be put together: Veterans need to learn how to build a new tribe, while their families and friends need to learn how to help them find a tribe that matters to them and pay that forward. Understanding PTSD and helping veterans find the proper treatment is absolutely key to helping them reintegrate and transition into their new tribe.

The Paradigm Shift of Your Tribe

Bob Proctor is best known for his book *You Were Born Rich* and his contribution to the movie *The Secret*, which expands on the idea of the Law of Attraction. Bob is a disciple of *Laws of Success* and *Think and Grow Rich*, both written by Napoleon Hill. Bob has studied thousands of books, by his own admission, continues to read *Think and Grow Rich* every day, and is considered the world's foremost expert on the human mind. I have attended several of his seminars, joined his Inner Circle, and implemented many of his teachings into my business through a process called "Thinking Into Results." I attribute much of my success in business and my personal life over the last few years to learning his guiding principles and putting them into practice.

Bob founded the Proctor Gallagher Institute along with Sandy Gallagher. Bob repeatedly drives the message, "Paradigms are a multitude of habits that guide every move you make. They affect the way you eat, the way you walk, even the way you talk. They govern your communication, your work habits, your successes, and your failures. For the most part, your paradigms didn't originate with you. They're the accumulated inheritance of other people's habits, opinions, and belief systems. Yet they remain the guiding force in YOUR life."[9]

In relation to veterans who are returning from duty, many of their paradigms were created by military training, their military leadership, the trauma they experienced, injuries they or close friends sustained,

9 https://www.proctorgallagherinstitute.com/1974/understanding-the-power-of-paradigms

and the influences of the brotherhood/sisterhood that surrounded them during their service. New paradigms replaced many of the paradigms they had before entering the military. How else would people go into battle, run toward the direction of bullets, or sacrifice their lives for others around them? How else would they become so singularly focused on the mission? The military calls it "training"; the mind looks at it as a newly created paradigm.

According to Dr. Maxwell Maltz, MD, FICS, author of *Psycho-Cybernetics*, the most important psychological discovery of the twentieth century was that of self-image. Each of us carries a mental blueprint or picture of ourselves. The picture dictates what we accept or reject as true in our lives. Our paradigms are a significant part of our self-image. All of our actions, behaviors, and beliefs are always in line with it. What's incredibly important is that our self-image can be changed, regardless of factors like age or social environment. No matter where we are in our lives, we have the power to change our paradigms and self-image. And that is at least partly what needs to happen to our veterans returning home after war.

The whole purpose of military training has been to completely reprogram each individual's self-image to allow them to succeed in their war-fighting missions and to do the things that most individuals would not normally do. The challenge comes when the service member leaves the military. Paradigms that worked for him or her while serving may no longer apply in the civilian world. For those returning soldiers, there is no "real life" boot camp to shift the paradigm and no drill sergeants screaming commands about opening up their softer side, finding a new tribe, sharing their feelings with their families, preventing isolation, or getting help from the VA when they really need it. Not happening. All are given a significant outbriefing with some very useful content, but the reinforcement and follow-up aren't there.

In a recent article in *New America's Weekly Wonk*, "What Vets Miss Most Is What Most Civilians Fear[10]: A Regimented, Cohesive Network That Always Checks on You," Mike Stajura, who joined the Army at seventeen, provided some great insight into the notion of the community of support in the military.

In the Army, it mattered to someone else whether or not my boots fit properly. It mattered to someone else whether I had been to the dentist recently. It mattered to someone else if I wasn't where I was supposed to be at the right time. (Believe me, I'd hear about it if I wasn't.)

That might sound odd to people who've never been in the military. Getting chewed out for not having your shoes shined hardly seems "supportive" to most people. But that's just one part of the military experience.

To be sure, all of this attention paid to my performance was in the interest of team performance, but it also meant someone was always there for me. Checking on me. Making sure I was good to go. All of us were doing this for one another. If I was on a road march and a member of my squad was struggling, I would help share his load. If I was on crutches and couldn't carry my tray in the dining hall, a fellow soldier would be right there to help me. That's just how it was. We learned to think of others first.

And then you exit the service.

In Stajura's comments, his sense of belonging was in the fact that other people cared about him and his service mattered to someone else. But things changed when he left the service. He needed a new set of paradigms and a new tribe to still feel recognized and valued. How do we create new paradigms when we don't know we need them, aren't really interested in learning new ones, and would rather have teeth extracted than try to express our feelings? One of the secrets is in the

---

10 http://www.businessinsider.com/what-veterans-miss-most-2013-11

last couple of sentences from Stajura's comments: *"We learned to think of others first."*

Focusing on Your New Tribe

To start shifting from isolation, shame, and depression, it helps to focus on others. The starting point for all happiness begins with shifting the focus away from yourself and to the outside instead. If you only think about yourself, you're going to be pretty miserable. Most people don't get up in the morning and give their first thought to how someone else is doing, but instead they are concerned with their own problems. However, true happiness results from caring about and focusing on others' needs. That's not something that comes naturally; you must learn how to do it.[11]

One handy tool to accomplish this is using gratitude. People in isolation tend to turn inward for answers. The problem? We don't have all the answers ourselves. We need others around us to fill in the gaps.

To reflect back on our paradigms, if we are "stuck" thinking about ourselves and the shame we feel or the wrongs we believe we've committed, we will probably establish a poor self-image and a set of bad habits (paradigms) to constantly reinforce these negative pictures of ourselves. According to Bob Proctor, to replace a paradigm, we must overlay a new one on top of the old one. That means we must create a new self-image and a new paradigm by training ourselves to use different tools. To be sure, some of these may sound too trivial to be meaningful. Certainly, no one tool will be a cure-all, but accumulating many simple new habits can create big changes. Just because the ideas are simple doesn't mean they're ineffective. Laugh them off at your own risk.

---

11 https://www.bible.com/reading-plans/937-habit-of-happiness/day/17#!

Let's choose a pretty simple new paradigm to work on first: gratitude. Start by writing down ten things you are grateful for on a daily basis. Don't just do it in your head. Write them down on paper each and every day. Gratitude can span intangible (such as good health, friendship, love) and tangible elements (such as a home, clothing, friends, and family). It can take about two minutes as you regularly do this, but the benefits are remarkably worthwhile. It's hard to feel self-loathing and personal shame when you are in the habit of being grateful for others around you. It is hard to be self-absorbed if you look for things to be grateful for. Gratitude helps reinforce positive emotions, brings good experiences to the forefront of memory, boosts happiness, and supports better relationship-building. It sounds so trivial—but what do you have to lose, other than two minutes of your time each day? If you need to, get someone else to do this along with you each day. Hold one another accountable for doing it. By working with others, you are starting to reach out and perhaps create a part of your new tribe.

The most important aspect of actively working on gratitude is the mental shift it causes. Instead of keeping a growing list of how you were wronged, how things didn't work out, or just negative events, keeping a gratitude list shifts the mind to look for more positives. It won't happen right away or even in a few weeks. It takes practice over a long time to cause this shift to be pronounced and permanent.

Of all the new habits you could develop after reading this book, gratitude for the blessings you have, the relationships you're in, and the simple positive occurrences throughout the day will help you realign your thinking to a positive outlook on life.

Remember, your old paradigms are powerful. Your self-image will actively work against your new approaches. You didn't learn to march on the first attempt, you weren't an excellent marksman your first time at the range, and you didn't learn all your mission skills in the first month of active duty. Only with concerted and repeated effort are new habits or paradigms made.

According to a UMass Dartmouth article,[12] researchers like Martin Seligman, Robert Emmons, and Michael McCullough are turning their attention to the study of gratitude and its relationship to health and mental well-being. Their research shows the following as quoted below:

- People who keep gratitude journals have been found to exercise more regularly, have fewer physical symptoms, feel better about their lives as a whole, and feel more optimistic about their upcoming week as compared to those who keep journals recording the stressors or neutral events of their lives.
- Daily discussion of gratitude results in higher reported levels of alertness, enthusiasm, determination, attentiveness, energy, and sleep duration and quality. Grateful people also report lower levels of depression and stress, although they do not deny or ignore the negative aspects of life.
- People who think about, talk about, or write about gratitude daily are more likely to report having helped someone with a personal problem or offered emotional support to another person.
- Those with a disposition toward gratitude are found to place less importance on material goods, are less likely to judge their own or others' success in terms of possessions accumulated, are less envious of wealthy people, and are more likely to share their possessions with others.

12 https://www.umassd.edu/counseling/for-parents/recommended-readings/the-importance-of-gratitude/

- Emerging research suggests that daily gratitude practices may even have some preventive benefits in warding off coronary artery disease.

So, what does this have to do with building a tribe after your service or deployment? In the end, the goal is to shift the paradigm of aloneness to a paradigm of belonging—in other words, trading our military tribe for a new tribe with a focus on our new civilian lives. The exercise might not seem to directly relate to building a new tribe, but it's a crucial piece of the puzzle: A habit of gratitude is a tool to create the environment to begin building one.

This whole change may sound difficult. In fact, you may even feel somewhat intimidated. It is a tremendous thought to consider the sheer magnitude of the transition from enlistment to civilian life. You are literally trading a band of brothers for your actual brothers and sisters. These people may be just the same as when you left them, but you are changed. You have seen and experienced things that few people in the world should have to experience. You have done it with a dedicated and similarly minded set of people by your side. That is not difficult to understand. But it is not always easy to simply trade in the guns and the battlefield for something that resembles a normal life.

So you, then, have to work on change. The world around you might remain the same, exactly how you left it. You have no control over that or those paradigms of the people to whom you return. They might simply think they are getting the same old John or Rachel that left them three years ago. They are mistaken, and that is okay. However, your happiness, success, and life are all ultimately your responsibility. If you do not address them quickly and replace the support you had from your previous tribe for the support you now need from your new one, you will feel isolated and start down a path no one should endure.

To help you recognize the paradigm shift, as well as the change that occurs as you transition from one tribe to another, let's look at the journey of two of our own, S.Sgt. Krause and Maj. Hall.

In Their Own Words

This section features the experiences of two people as they transitioned away from the military. As you read these stories, pay attention to how both experiences were greatly impacted by the tribe of people around them. For S.Sgt. Meg Krause, her tribe was her reserve unit after she deployed in an active-duty unit. She mattered to these people and together, they made sure she received the treatment she needed.

In the second case, Maj. Hall pushed his family away. The strong love of his wife, who refused to give up, and her tenacity to reach out to the major's commanding officer led to his revival.

In both cases, their tribe made the difference and likely saved their lives. In both cases, it was also true that neither of them realized that they were part of these tribes. In fact, both tried to leave their unit or family. That's a powerful thing to realize.

Staff Sergeant Meg Krause[13]

Meg: I am Staff Sergeant Meg Krause. I was on active duty for five years. I joined the reserves, so I came off active duty and now I am the noncommissioned officer in charge of a battalion aid station for a combat engineering unit in Pennsylvania. Operation Iraqi Freedom, I flew combat casualty missions, so we picked patients up and flew them

13 https://www.coursehero.com/file/p521ddo1/As-an-Army-medic-Staff-Sargent-Meg-Krause-knew-the-warning-signs-of-depression/

from Baghdad back to Germany for medical care. I was "stop-lossed" in 2006; I would have gotten out of the service, but I was deployed to Iraq at the time just outside of Tikrit. I was a medic. We got mortared a lot, and we always say that when everybody else has to turn away and pull security, we have to turn around and face the damage. My psychological health ... I didn't think it was an issue when I came home. I would tell myself, "I am going to be okay. I am not going to be one of those people who clams up and doesn't talk about it and can't handle it." It wasn't until two and a half years later, when I was in the high stress of graduating from college, writing papers, taking tests, looking for a job, looking for an apartment, everything I have worked for, for goodness knows how many years, is coming to a close and I don't even know what I am doing next and that is when I really started to notice a problem.

Sgt. McCarthy: When I first got to the unit, she was very driven, dedicated, always wanting to be here, always looking out for her soldiers.

Sgt. Young: Very outgoing. She was the kind of person that wanted to tackle all the missions.

1st Sgt. Renninger: Very dependable person, very knowledgeable. Always working with her soldiers.

Sgt. Young: After about six, seven months after Sergeant Krause came to this unit, I noticed she was sleeping a lot. I was having to call her a lot because she was late. She was very irritable.

Sgt. McCarthy: She just became disinterested and not really wanting to be a part of the team anymore.

Meg: I think that I was the last person to notice that there was a lot of alcohol, a lot of alcohol involved, and I always just wrote it off as, "I am in college, this is what you do. Who cares if I am twenty-six years old and I am drinking a bottle of wine in the evening just to get to sleep and have a nightmare here or there?" I figured it was normal, and

I would just avoid any triggers that gave me flashbacks. But one of my soldiers actually sat me down over lunch and said, "You know, Sergeant Krause, you know as well as I do, I mean we are medics ... you know the signs and symptoms of depression."

Sgt. Young: I said, "You might be suffering from PTSD. I think you need to get it checked out." So I went through all the symptoms that I thought she was exhibiting and I said, "I really think it would benefit you and us as a medical section to get it checked out."

Meg: Then there was another incident at my unit where one day when I was on drill weekend, I just said, "Forget this," and I did not go to formation. Sergeant McCarthy, who is my first-line supervisor, what he said to me when I finally answered the phone was, "Well, why don't you just come in and talk to us?" He said, "Talk to First Sergeant. I have seen him talk to people about this before. He understands." And so I came in and First Sergeant sat me down and said, "You know, I remember the smell of the 50 cal," and we talked for a while. At the end of it, we were joking and laughing and it was still First Sarge and I was still Staff Sergeant Krause, and I am still in my medical section and he was okay with that.

1st Sgt. Renninger: I knew something was wrong with her and the possibility of PTSD when she did come back from Iraq and joined our unit, reason being is because I came back from Iraq in 2005 and I had PTSD too. And that is how I know the symptoms of what Sergeant Krause is going through. I have all the respect for her in the world, and that goes for all the rest of my soldiers that are in this unit.

Meg: The VA hospital did something that was really amazing that no one else was able to do and what that was [was to] give me the help I needed, exactly when I needed it and in a manner that made sense to me. What I wish more warriors would realize is that I was getting worse and worse and worse because I didn't go get help. The problem just got bigger and bigger and bigger and one little thing that you think you can handle suddenly grows into this giant pile of I don't even know what to eat; and if I had just gotten help six months before I did, I would have really been better off in the long run. Because it wasn't until I got the emotional help that I needed that I was able to fix the rest of my problems.

Sgt. McCarthy: She is back to the way she was when I first got in the unit as far as being a very dedicated NCO to her soldiers, the mission, training. She is a very outstanding NCO. I think it takes quite a bit of strength in order to admit that you have an issue but it also takes the intuitiveness of a friend, a leader, supervisor, to pick up on the signal that the soldier is having issues and needs to seek professional help in dealing with it.

Meg: I think it shows real strength when someone admits that they need help and gets it even if they don't want to.

Major Jeff Hall[14]

Jeff: My name is Major Jeff Hall. I've been in the Army for seventeen years.

Sgt. Anthony Bingham: Major Hall was my battery commander for Operation Iraqi Freedom 1 and 3. If he said that we were going to storm the gates of hell today, I would say, "All right, sir, let's go."

Jeff: The first deployment when we entered Baghdad, the people were really glad to see us. It seemed like the year just flew by. We captured a lot of people that needed to be captured. It just seemed like we could do our job. It was the second tour that I started to really feel it grinding down on me. I couldn't find anything that we were doing that was advancing the ball down the field. We essentially were driving around

14 https://www.brainline.org/video/real-warriors-maj-jeff-hall

until we got blown up. We had an IED incident where two of the guys that were in my tank unit that was attached to me were killed, and one of the lieutenants was wounded severely. I don't know why, but that shook me. It really shook me to the bone. I had seen dead GIs before. I've held a couple of guys as the chopper came into pick them up. I just always was able to troop on, but for some reason, it was like the straw that broke the camel's back for me, and my anger started to really come out.

Sheri Hall (Wife): I could tell when he walked in the door of the hangar he wasn't the same man. He would say things, and his eyes would get black. He would have a deep, dark look in his eyes. That was not Jeff at all. We just kept hoping that things would get better, but they weren't.

Jeff: The impact on the girls, when I came back, I became more and more distant. I used to do everything with them. That all ended. That was not important to me anymore. I didn't want them to be part of what was going on with me. I looked at my bike to just get away from everybody. I'd get on it, and I would literally ride 1,000 miles. My back was just killing me by the time I got off it, and I didn't care, the further I could go. If I could have driven it [sic] into the ocean at that time, I would have, but in the deepest throes of the depression that hit me I stopped riding it altogether. I was going to sell the bike. I didn't need it anymore. I was selling off all my possessions. I didn't want anything anymore.

Sheri: I worried. I never, ever worried before until he started telling me, "I just want you to go away. Take everything; take the kids and just go away." I knew I couldn't leave him alone.

Jeff: I started viewing suicide as a way to just stop. I was just wanting to turn off the 600 TV sets that were going on in my head all the time. I couldn't handle it no more [sic]. I started having suicide ideations to the point where I was actually in the backyard with a pistol thinking about killing myself. The only thing that really stopped me was thinking, *My God, my kids are going to come home from school and find me this way.*

Col. Daniel Pinnell: Jeff's frustration and anger really reached a peak. At the same time, his wife expressed to my wife concern and then to me directly that Jeff was very negative at home. He seems hopeless; he does not see a path to the future. As soon as I had that cue plus my own personal interaction with Jeff, his decreasing physical performance on the job, I knew that we had to take him for professional care. Basically, what I did is called directly over to mental health. I saw them, and I told them, "If you're not able to help him immediately, if you are not capable of making this happen here, then you need to call me immediately. If he's not cooperative or doesn't show up, contact me immediately. I will be involved in this until we get him to the person or place that we need."

Jeff: It wasn't until Colonel Pinnell noticed and helped me find the right person on Fort Hope. Colonel Pinnell knew about the program in Washington, DC, the Deployment Health Clinical Center. He recommended that I go to that. It felt like the cat was out of the bag, and there was no way I could put it back in. I was like, "You know what? I'm going to do it." Believe it or not, about 100 pounds of weight came off me right then.

Sheri: It wasn't until he came back from his evaluation with the DHCC that he was really excited about the program that I started to see a little bit of hope in his eyes. He asked me to go with him. That was hopeful for me because at that point I didn't know where we were going to be by the end of the year.

Jeff: Sheri spent group time with us where she could hear other soldiers saying the same thing that I was saying. She was able to understand there are some pretty dark holes there and for me to understand that she sat back home worried to death about me, trying to stay strong, trying to have a face for the rest of the family who was constantly asking, "How's Jeff doing?," and not knowing because I don't call. I could see the stress on her and the strain. We came to a middle ground where we could start talking about these things, and it helped us. I will tell you that I think PTSD will grab hold of you without you even knowing it, but I don't think it's an animal that can't be killed. I think that you can defeat it, but you can't do it on your own.

Jeff: I tried to ignore it, and it came back probably tenfold on me because of that. If you ever make it to a two-way program like the DHCC, you're going to see colonels. You're going to see sergeant first classes and sergeant majors in this program. I'm starting to see at the higher levels of command they're understanding, "Wow, we owe these guys a chance to heal." Don't be afraid to come forward if you have troubles.

Building a Tribe

It doesn't take long for veterans to become disenchanted with the way things are after they return from their service. The world of politics, race relations, general disunity within personal relationships, and the overall imperfect world can become disheartening. This disheartening feeling needs to be replaced with thoughts of what unites us. We are a very resilient people. But we cannot do this alone. We all need a respective tribe. It is literally our lifeline. To that end, this chapter will help you build your tribe and reconnect with the people who love you, care for you, and want you to succeed in reconnecting with your happiness.

Chapter 3

BUILDING A HEALTHY LIFE AFTER SERVICE:

Forgiveness, Healing, and Recovery

As I write this chapter, we are approaching the New Year. Television commercials are already hitting the airwaves with promises of healthy living through new exercise equipment, newly discovered diets, and all kinds of ways to implement New Year's resolutions. We've all seen them, and if we've gained enough weight over the holidays we might even try some of these innovations. But, we also know that many of these are just gimmicks to prod us into a purchase to soothe our guilty souls as we enter another year.

Unfortunately, even with the purchase of a new Fitbit, Simply Fit board, the new version of P90X, or whatever the year's best fitness toys might be, how to use them still remains a personal decision. For the most part, many of our best intentions fall by the wayside in a month or two after we dedicate ourselves to the resolution. I do have to say though, sticking to a program and doing P90X last year gave me the best shot at climbing to 11,000 feet to fulfill my dream of elk hunting in Colorado. So all is not lost.

But to this point, have you ever felt that everyone around you offers—at most times unsolicited—health advice and tips? Between friends and family, healthcare providers, and the media, we are bombarded by healthy living "opportunities." Intellectually speaking, we all realize the importance of eating well, exercising regularly, not drinking excessively, and not smoking. But many of us feel overwhelmed in our hectic lives, and it's easy to get off track.

That's been my struggle in writing this chapter. I aim to convey an important message without making you feel like I'm selling you something. The truth though is that I can't write anything that is going to convince anybody to do something that they sincerely don't want to do; but I can provide some information to help you better understand the impact of those decisions and learn about some common challenges veterans face in their return home, from the perspective of one who has walked this path.

This chapter isn't a cure-all, but it does contain some interesting information about how critical our thinking is to creating a healthy lifestyle. I haven't seen many commercials on the importance of forgiveness or the need for a new way of thinking to diminish depression or other conditions common with returning vets.

A growing body of literature has found a link between trauma and physical health.[15] Those who report that they have significant challenges in mentally adjusting after service are more likely to have a greater number of physical health problems than those who do not have the

15 http://www.ptsd.va.gov/professional/treat/cooccurring/ptsd_physical_health.asp

same types of issues. Veterans utilizing VHA services were almost fifteen times more likely to have poor health status than the general population and fourteen times more likely to have five or more medical conditions than the general population. Among the most prevalent medical conditions found in veteran patients are high blood pressure and heart conditions. Other common conditions include diabetes, chronic lung disease, depression, and alcohol-related problems.

Current thinking is that the experience of trauma brings about neurochemical changes in the brain. These changes likely have biological as well as psychological and behavioral effects on the health of returning veterans. I've seen this theory in action time and time again. The psychological and behavioral effects on health may be accounted for in part by depressive and anxiety disorders veterans experience when returning from combat. Depressed individuals report a greater number of physical symptoms and use more medical treatment than individuals who are not depressed.

Regardless, veterans need to recognize the health risks posed by their combat experiences. Then, they should understand that they could take preventive actions to avoid unhealthy outcomes. Similar to how basic training prepared each young recruit to be ready for battle, it is possible to take action to create a healthier future. Focusing on self-forgiveness and healthy living habits can help veterans overcome this seeming predisposition to these sad statistics. And, for those who fall behind the eight ball and feel trapped in a precarious lifestyle filled with bitterness and anger, there is a road map to recovery. There is no reason to fall prey to the feelings of self-loathing, self-punishment, and an unfulfilled life.

Remember, you don't need to be diagnosed with PTSD to be depressed, have a substance abuse problem, or struggle in coping with certain parts of your life. This chapter will provide veterans with some tools to recognize a different reality and the possibilities of full recovery from whatever haunts their minds after combat.

The Importance of Forgiving

Anthony de Mello was a spiritual leader, author, and psychotherapist. He said, "There is only one cause of unhappiness: the false beliefs you have in your head, beliefs so widespread, so commonly held, that it never occurs to you to question them." Many veterans return from combat with a belief that they could have done something different, said something different, or somehow could have changed an outcome. In their minds, the fault lies squarely on their own shoulders. These thoughts create a false narrative in their minds, which causes feelings of guilt and self-doubt to permeate almost all aspects of their lives. Their minds constantly search for thoughts or other evidence that feeds into these false beliefs. It's as though they believe that they are Superman and could have altered every possible outcome and prevented each and every harm.

With all the training we receive, it's hard not to believe we can do anything. We can fly through AAA fire; we can pull a buddy out of the line of fire when he's hurt; we are willing to run toward the enemy's incoming bullets. It's really tough to sometimes admit we couldn't do something we now believe we should have. It's hard to understand how some survived and others didn't. And many times, there is no one around to offer forgiveness. For many veterans, if it were offered, they might not even want to accept it. But forgiveness is an essential part of the recovery process. Indeed, forgiveness is one of the most important words for vets returning home.

Generally speaking, vets face two primary types of forgiveness:

1. Forgiving themselves for their perceived actions or inactions during their deployments overseas.

2. Forgiving others who they perceive have either wronged them or harmed them. This can include family/friends who don't understand their challenges during their transition to their civilian lives, the rest of the world for not acting in a rational/ethical way and fully supporting the sacrifice they made; and, of course, forgiving the enemy.

Unresolved guilt, whether for actual or perceived offenses, can hinder or prevent well-being, trauma recovery, a normal progression through life, productive action, and positive relationships. Recognized or unrecognized guilt can undermine relationships over prolonged periods or affect the kinds of relationships a person attracts to himself or herself. It can keep the guilt-ridden individual "stuck" in suffering, depression, and/or self-recrimination.[16] Forgiveness takes time, effort, and energy, and can be one of the most difficult acts a person undertakes.

Whether guilt is generated within ourselves or requires the forgiveness of others, the most important aspect is that forgiveness is a healing power. To withhold forgiveness does nothing beneficial for either you or the party needing the forgiveness. Forgiveness is an internal force and leads to a path of recovery. The key is to be aware of the sources of self-created guilt and fight it as though it were your enemy—because it is. As Paulo Coelho, author of *The Alchemist* states: "You don't drown by falling into a river, but by staying submerged in it."

Self-Forgiveness

Self-forgiveness is a process of rewriting your thoughts (false beliefs) into a realistic story that recognizes the truth and the humanness of each person. It starts the process of creating a new life that is better suited

16 https://www.giftfromwithin.org/html/Guilt-Following-Traumatic-Events.html

for the memories of all of those who have made sacrifices. Survival is not a sin; in fact, survival is a blessing. It is a tragedy that so many have been killed or injured, but it is a blessing to all of us that were not killed. Although choices may be limited during a traumatic event, the survivor does have choices after the event. She or he can remain locked in numbness or distress or can use survival as a source of insight and growth.

Many times, false beliefs hold us back from self-forgiveness. While these feelings of guilt and shame feel so personal and individual, they are incredibly common among returning veterans. There is a commonality to how veterans have been rewired through their training to react with such similar responses. A very important aspect of improving the quality of your life is to recognize that you are not the only person feeling this way. Your false beliefs are constructed in very similar ways amongst your entire peer group of veterans. You are not alone

Judeo-Christian principles generally teach that no one should murder other human beings. However, military personnel are trained to be agents of death.[17] Extremely powerful, vivid internal pressures accumulate on individuals in a war zone. Coupled with repeatedly threatening situations and an accumulation of traumatic experiences and losses, some veterans explode into acts of which they are not proud or may be ashamed. When errors in human judgment or in the execution of duties occur, resulting deaths and injuries typically invoke severe reactions of guilt and shame and/or profound denial of any adverse emotional reactions.

At the time of the trauma, a quick and immediate sense arises that one should respond according to "ordinary" standards, in certain constructive ways, by stopping the trauma or evil or by helping other people. None of these may be possible during extreme trauma. At the very best,

17 https://citeseerx.ist.psu.edu/viewdoc/download?doi=10.1.1.196.6317&rep=rep1&type=pdf

the possible response is less than the ideal. The reaction to this compromised response can be perpetual self-condemnation.

When endangered, the body responds in a neurochemical manner to propel us to protective action (counter-aggression, stillness, or flight). Survival becomes an emotional imperative. During and after traumatic events, individuals often must find immediate ways to survive. In the chaos, arousal, and propulsion to self-protect, we may act in ways that we later regret.

At individual points in time, guilt is a common reaction when someone close dies even under normal circumstances. This is true even if we had a negative connection with the person. We always have regrets after someone dies—things said or not said, done or not done. Then there is the guilt of a survivor, a sense that they should have sacrificed their own lives to save others, or their thoughts about their own survival. But in truth, this is an opportunity to honor the deceased and others who are close to us by valuing life and relationships and behaving accordingly.

Trauma or death may intensify—or produce—guilt. For example, you may experience a little guilt or discomfort if a friend asked you to come talk and you did not get there before he or she left town. A war veteran described intense and persistent guilt after he failed to arrive in time to hear the last words of his close friend who had been urgently asking for him.

After traumatic events, guilt may be a part of an ongoing sense of helplessness and/or ineffectualness. Often, people who have experienced a traumatic event are particularly troubled by the fact that they could not exert control over what was happening.

Individuals with a sense of responsibility for those around them may be particularly vulnerable to feelings of guilt. Among this group are individuals in positions of authority or leadership. Those professionals charged with rescuing or maintaining the well-being of others (e.g., medics) habitually feel responsible for the outcome of others. For some, responsibility for others is defined as part of the job. Often, people readily relinquish responsibility to these individuals, adding to the sense that it is their charge not only to keep things right but to make things right. As a result, members of this group may feel a sense of failure and guilt in the absence of a positive outcome.

On February 10, 2017, Gen. Hal Moore died. He was a legendary military commander who, as a lieutenant colonel, became infamous in the Battle of Ia Drang on November 14, 1965. This battle was the US military's first major engagement in the Vietnam War and the war's bloodiest battle.

The story of this battle was documented in a book called *We Were Soldiers Once ... and Younger* and then produced into a similarly named movie starring Mel Gibson in the role of Lt. Col. Hal Moore. Gen. Moore shares the story of how he and his 457 men suddenly found themselves up against thousands of North Vietnamese soldiers.

At the end of the battle, more than 200 American soldiers had died and approximately the same number were wounded. However, the enemy lost an estimated 3,000 soldiers in the battle. By every account, Gen. Moore's heroic actions exposed him to intense enemy fire to ensure that he could lead the proper deployment of his unit in the face of overwhelming odds. He refused to leave the battlefield to brief generals on at least three separate occasions. As described by others, if there was a person to lead in combat, it was Hal Moore.

In 1992, Gen. Moore, who had retired in 1977, conducted an interview on NPR's radio program *Fresh Air* with Terry Gross.[18] I listened to a replay of the interview on the day of his death. His story gives great

18 https://www.npr.org/2017/02/15/515387382/remembering-lt-gen-harold-moore-heroic-vietnam-war-commander

insight into the environment he faced during that battle and the enormous responsibility he felt for the care of his men. But, more importantly, I noted the guilt he carried. "Every day," he said, he replayed the events of that day and wondered what he could have done differently. Every day, he worried about the souls of the men he lost under his command. Incredibly, even years after the battle, it was the survivors who brought him comfort in their words of support. The following is a brief excerpt from the interview.

MOORE: I didn't get any sleep. Along about the, oh, early morning of the third day, my mind was still functioning clearly and cleanly and quickly, due that on adrenaline or just on training and stamina. But the curious thing that happened was that I had to think every word before I would say it into the radio or to people around me. It was like translating English into English, if you can understand what I'm trying to say.

... The thing I thought about was my troopers on the ground and accomplishing my mission. And I never gave a thought, in any fight I've ever been in, in two wars, whether or not I'd get hit. If I got hit, I got hit. That's it. My job was to lead troops. And to lead them, you got to be on the battlefield, and you cannot be fearful. You got to keep your cool. And I never knelt down.

And never in my head—it never crossed my mind that we would go down in that fight against great odds. I knew in my heart that we would prevail. We had massive fire support. We had disciplined troops. And we were tough. And we were good. It never entered my mind to make a personal bargain with God for me or for my men. I knew we'd win.

GROSS: General, when bombs are falling and there's artillery fire all around and you're under attack, this is a—you know, the question of somebody who's never served or been in battle, but how do you think clearly? I mean, this is the time when you are most required to think clearly but when it must be most difficult to do so.

MOORE: I really have never had any problem thinking clearly in a tough time, critical situation. I think I kind of go into a sort of a zone and blank out all the horrible brutality which is going on around me, being aware of it nevertheless but realizing that I was a commander—I am a commander—and I am responsible for preserving as many American lives as I can and killing as many enemy as I can.

Now, in the smoke and the dust, which limits visibility and the terrible heat—that compounds the situation. The men screaming and yelling, giving orders in three languages—English, Spanish, Vietnamese; wounded men screaming for medics and for their mother, about to die—I've never found it difficult to keep my head in situations like that. I'm a paratrooper. I've had a couple of malfunctions. Once, I was eight seconds from hitting the ground, but I knew I'd make it in on my reserve if I could get it open. So I've never really been concerned when I've been in tough situations. Just do the job.

GROSS: I guess you can't allow yourself to get too emotional about your men dying in the middle of a fight.

MOORE: No, you cannot. And furthermore, you cannot impart, by your very manner and your voice on the radio, any possible sign or word or tone of voice that would indicate to any listener or any of your men looking at you that you were rattled. You had to look cool and be cool. And it's something you can't put on.

GROSS: What about when the battle's over and you don't have to be cool and you don't have to be unemotional, does it get you in a different way then?

MOORE: Yep. That's when it's always hit me. In this battle, I looked around on the ground and saw some of my—many of my precious men in their ponchos, lying dead, men whom I have trained for eighteen months—knew their wives, children, many of them—knew them very closely. And I knew a terrible truth that, twenty-four hours later, would shatter the hearts of their families back home in America. And that got to me. Darn right, it did.

And I—never a day goes by, in the twenty-seven years since that battle, that I don't refight it in my mind and think about those great Americans who never backed off, many of them who had only seven to ten days left in the service. And they went home in coffins. And I'm forever grateful for their service, and I grieve for them forever. And for years, I felt guilty that I was not killed. I guess that's a normal reaction from a commander who loves his men.

GROSS: You don't feel that way anymore?

MOORE: I've kind of gotten over it a little bit. A few years back, several of my troopers told me at one of these reunions, they said Colonel—and they still call me Colonel, which is fine—Colonel, you got to stop feeling that way because if you died in that place, none of us would have got out of there.

Well, I don't know if that's true or false, but that made me feel better.

"If only ..." are the words that create self-loathing, self-condemnation, and a process of rumination, which is repetitively thinking about the causes, situational factors, and consequences of one's negative emotional experience. It is our own version of the Monday morning quarterback practice. It's always easy to see different possibilities at ground speed zero. Our ability to second-guess ourselves has wreaked more havoc on the minds of veterans than perhaps any other behavior. Rumination is the author of self-hate. Rumination rewrites history in a way that produces a list of should-haves and could-haves. These rewrites are the "false beliefs" that prevent our happiness.

Newly created false beliefs and guilt may be a complicated result of experiencing traumatic events. Guilt may result in hopelessness, depression, and other problems, such as self-harm, suicidal feelings, and substance abuse.

This all adds up to one thing: We're not in control of all aspects of our surrounding world. We don't have a crystal ball that tells us with certainty that the outcomes would have been different if we'd reacted in a different way. We are not supermen or superwomen. So, the only solution for all of this? Forgiveness. And, since nobody else probably even knows you are struggling with these thoughts, you're the only one who can offer this forgiveness—self-forgiveness.

Self-forgiveness is the sword that will pierce the spirit of guilt to ensure this cruel oppressor will no longer rule your life. Intentionally or unintentionally, most of us committed acts or failed to act, causing pain to another person. The range of offenses varies from slight (hurt feelings) to severe spiritual, emotional, or physical harm to others (disrupted life or death).

Many studies into the relationship between forgiveness and one's own health exist. The most important point? The general consensus that self-forgiveness is inversely related to depression and suicide. People who harbor chronic negative emotions associated with self-condemnation report higher levels of depression, anxiety, and hostility as well as lower levels of life satisfaction, well-being, and positive experiences. By practicing self-forgiveness, you place yourself on a course moving away from depression, anxiety, and hostility. While suicidal behaviors are on the extreme, everyone coping with any transition needs to create better life satisfaction, well-being, and a positive attitude. Practicing self-forgiveness helps you accomplish just that.

Even after many years, I still deal with this need for self-forgiveness. I'm so incredibly hard on myself. The stress of combat and the way I dealt with it at the time put additional stress on my crew. We were all under stress, but I hold myself accountable for some of it, things said or not said. I have so much admiration for my crewmates. They were the best to be with. I never really took the time to tell them.

I also suppose it is related to how long I waited to seek help. I regret the times I've lost my temper and failed to be the person I want to be. I know that I've created some false beliefs in my mind, and I react negatively to them on occasion. I simply just keep trying to rewrite the narrative, replacing the negative beliefs with positive thoughts of who I am now. I try not to accept the guilt. I reject it.

The most important part is to recognize the negative behaviors or thoughts, acknowledge that you no longer need to suffer, and to move forward in a more positive way. Whether you tell yourself that "He or she wouldn't want me to suffer anymore," "I'm not the same person as I was then," or "I will live my life in a way to honor him/her"—whatever it is, choose the appropriate phrase and repeat it, without fail, every time you feel guilty. In this way, you are not only telling yourself the truth—that you are no longer the person who committed a past misdeed—you are also giving your brain a new, more positive input. This will help wean it off the old wiring that keeps messaging guilt long after guilt is deserved.

Be aware of any desire to self-punish. To do so, consider the following:

- Self-punishment is nonproductive; take positive action instead.
- Avoid eliciting self-punishment, even by demeanor.
- Avoid putting yourself in a position to be punished, rejected, or demeaned.
- Take positive action that benefits the offended.

The Road to Healing

Whatever your feelings may be, do not condemn yourself to a life sentence of self-hatred after returning home from your service. A path to recovery and a road to healing exist. You can move through this and find a better place. Each veteran can overcome these challenges and live a healthy, enjoyable life.

No matter how long the VA wait times or how isolated or emotionally cut off from others you feel, know that you're not alone and that you can do *plenty* things to start feeling better. You can learn to deal with nightmares and flashbacks, cope with feelings of depression, anxiety, or guilt, and restore your sense of control. To wit, the following interview with Dr. Beth Dietzel should further explain and address these feelings and emotions that many of our veterans face as they return to civilian life.

In Her Own Words; Interview between the author and Dr. Beth Dietzel, PhD

Dr. Beth Dietzel, PhD, Clinical Psychologist at Battle Creek VA Medical Center

BOB: Why did you decide to become a psychologist and work with veterans through the VA?

DR. DIETZEL: I have always been drawn to helping others, listening to people while offering a safe space for them to share. I was especially impacted by a college professor who shared his experiences working with patients doing therapy. I recall feeling connected with his stories and wanting to be part of that, in some capacity. I have family members who have served in the military, so the VA seemed to be a natural fit for me, allowing me to give back to those who have served our country.

BOB: Is there one thing you would want a veteran who is reading this book to also consider?

DR. DIETZEL: I believe the therapeutic relationship is critical in one's journey of healing. If a veteran is meeting with a therapist and not feeling well connected, I hope he/she chooses to share this with the therapist so they can discuss options moving forward. These options may include an adjustment with the current therapist, creating a better working relationship with him/her, or discussing a transfer to another therapist. Veterans need to feel comfortable and psychologically safe to share with their individual therapist for them to get the most out of therapy, so I would want them to know it is appropriate to have this discussion with their therapist and to consider a transfer to another therapist if necessary.

BOB: This book talks about sleep being one of the most important aspects of health for a veteran. Do you agree with that? Why/why not?

DR. DIETZEL: Absolutely. If an individual is not sleeping well, it affects a myriad of areas in his/her life, including mood, processing speed, digestion, energy, and concentration, just to name a few. Many of the veterans with whom I have worked have struggled with sleep for years. That has a significant impact, and addressing it in treatment ought to be a central part of their treatment plan.

BOB: What do you think would be the three most important issues facing veterans in their transitions relating to their mental well-being?

DR. DIETZEL: That is a great question and different for each veteran going through this process. Generally speaking, I believe several veterans transitioning out of the military face challenges regarding (1) sense of purpose, (2) sense of identity, and (3) communication and feeling understood.

BOB: This book is *not* intended to take the place of professional mental healthcare. What would you recommend for a veteran to do who is struggling with their transition from military life to civilian life?

DR. DIETZEL: I would encourage them to reach out, to get connected with their VA. This may seem overwhelming to people, especially if it's their first time speaking with a mental health professional or their first time connecting with the VA. The VA has mental health professionals embedded in primary care, so if veterans are participating in primary care through the VA, they may request to speak with a mental health professional during such a visit and a warm handoff may occur that same day. Veterans may present as a "walk-in" as well, allowing them to speak with a mental health care provider the same day. If a veteran is not connected with a VA, he/she would need to register with the VA before services occur.

BOB: What is the most rewarding experience you've had in treating a veteran? Obviously, you can't share a patient's name or confidential information, but is there a general story you can share?

DR. DIETZEL: It is an honor to be part of a veteran's journey in his/her recovery. I recall comments from veterans such as "I didn't realize this is what 'good sleep' felt like" and "I have more options now. I can go places and do things with my family." Comments such as those are very rewarding. That's an awesome thing to be part of in one's life.

BOB: Where has the VA made the most progress in mental health in the last ten years?

DR. DIETZEL: There are three areas in mental health I want to highlight here: The first two are focused on the VA as a whole, and the third is focused on information from my local VA. First, the VA's decision to embed psychologists, mental health professionals, in primary care clinics was especially prudent. Mental health care is still surrounded by stigma, unfortunately, and the VA's decision to create an option for a literal warm handoff from a primary care provider to a mental health provider was innovative and has allowed so many more veterans to learn more about their mental health and options for mental health care within the VA.

Second, the VA has led the way with virtual care, offering veterans video appointments with their providers. This has become more evident to people over the spring of 2020, during the COVID-19 pandemic, though the VA had been offering such options to veterans for years already and was able to shift more smoothly during that time. Third, my local VA took steps to pool resources for veterans participating in residential care. Rather than providers working with veterans in one specific residential program, we identified several group offerings that could be beneficial for veterans participating in a variety of programs, so providers could offer groups and classes to veterans across residential programs. We created "VA University" (VAU for short) about five to ten years ago, allowing us to offer a wider variety of classes and groups for veterans in our residential programs. Veterans in our residential programs have some program-specific groups and classes and then others (VAU) that they elect to participate in based on individual needs at the time.

Dr. Dietzel offers some excellent guidance on how veterans can rely on the VA and its professionals to offer substantial and remarkable care to heal from their experiences. In addition to working with the VA, some self-care steps should be taken. They are in no way a means of avoiding or delaying care provided by the VA; rather, they are an added means of improving one's own mental health.

In addition to self-forgiveness, several almost universally accepted steps exist on the road to healing. I'll stick with the very basics:[19]

1. Get moving.
2. Don't isolate yourself.

19 http://www.helpguide.org/articles/ptsd-trauma/ptsd-in-veterans.htm

3. Self-regulate your nervous system.
4. Make choices that will boost your physical health.

Step 1: Get Moving.

As well as helping to burn off adrenaline, exercise can release endorphins and make you feel better. By *really focusing* on how your body feels as you exercise, you can start to reprogram your nervous system. Rhythmic exercise—such as running, swimming, basketball, or even dancing—engages your arms and legs and works well if, instead of continuing to focus on your thoughts as you exercise, you focus on how your body feels. Rock climbing, boxing, weight training, or martial arts can make it easier to focus on your movements. It's like riding a motorcycle or, for me, flying a plane. When I fly privately, I don't have any choice but to pay strict attention to my flying. Riding a motorcycle does the same thing for me. It takes my mind off other things. Pursuing outdoor activities like hiking, camping, mountain biking, rock climbing, whitewater rafting, and skiing can challenge your sense of vulnerability and help you transition back into civilian life.

Step 2: Don't Isolate Yourself

Connecting with others face-to-face doesn't have to mean a lot of talking. Every veteran should find someone who will listen without judging when they want to talk or who will just hang out with them when they don't. That person may be your significant other, a family member, one of your service buddies, or a civilian friend.

You may feel like the civilians in your life can't understand you since they haven't been in the service or experienced what you have. But people's experiences don't have to mirror yours; they can still offer you support. What matters is that they care about you, are a good listener, and are a source of comfort.

Step 3: Self-Regulate Your Nervous System

When you feel agitated, anxious, or out of control, know that you can change your aggravation and calm yourself. Consider these ways to do so:

Mindful Breathing. To quickly calm yourself in any situation, take sixty breaths, focusing on each breath in and out.

Sensory Input. Just as loud noises, certain smells, or the feel of sand in your clothes can instantly transport you back to the combat zone, sensory input can quickly calm you. Everyone responds a little differently, so experiment to find out what works best for you. Think back to your time on deployment and consider: What brought you comfort at the end of the day? Perhaps it was looking at photos of your family? Or listening to a favorite song? Smelling a certain brand of soap? Petting an animal?

Reconnect Emotionally. By reconnecting to uncomfortable emotions without becoming overwhelmed, you can make a huge difference in your ability to manage stress, balance your moods, and take back control of your life.

Step 4: Make Choices That Will Boost Your Physical Health

Without the rush of still being in a combat zone, you may feel strange or even dead inside and find it difficult to relax. Many veterans are drawn to things that offer a familiar adrenaline rush, whether it's caffeine, drugs, violent video games, driving recklessly, or daredevil sports. These stresses can be hard on your body and mind, so make sleep, healthy food, and calming activities a priority. Let's focus on some healthy habits for veterans returning from overseas that include the following:

Take time to relax with relaxation techniques such as massage, meditation, or yoga.

Avoid alcohol and drugs (including nicotine). It can be tempting to turn to drugs and alcohol to numb painful feelings and memories and get to sleep. But substance abuse (and cigarettes) can make the symptoms worse.

Find safe ways to blow off steam. Pound on a punching bag, pummel a pillow, sing along to loud music, or find a secluded place to scream at the top of your lungs.

Support your body with a healthy diet. Omega-3s play a vital role in emotional health, so incorporate food such as fatty fish, flaxseed, and walnuts into your diet. Limit processed and fried food, sugars, and refined carbs, which can exacerbate mood swings and energy fluctuations.

Get plenty of sleep. Sleep deprivation exacerbates anger, irritability, and moodiness. Aim for somewhere between seven to nine hours of sleep each night.

The Path to Recovery

I certainly concede that all of this is easier said than done. But none of these tips and resources are unreachable or considered difficult. It simply takes effort and dedication to eventually transform them into your daily habits and rituals. So many variables exist in how each veteran handles his or her return from deployment. Some feel the impact almost immediately, while others like S.Sgt. Meg Krause didn't have significant problems until two years had passed.

That's a really important point in this whole approach. You can't wait until you're having problems. If you do, it could be too late. You have to be proactive. When I was trained in the B-52, we had to learn how to operate with degraded avionics. In spite of having triple inertial navigation computers, we had to prepare to deliver our weapons even when our systems had completely malfunctioned. Our leaders recognized that you couldn't wait for a system malfunction to prepare for it. That said, just like in your service, you must adjust to circumstances to overcome adversity. Waiting to react is tantamount to preparing to fail. The key is to understand your current circumstances and understand how best to move forward. Don't just let events unfold without being prepared and educated about them. The following war story should help you better recognize this:

War Story: 12 out of 10

(Combat Experience—Gen. Schwarzkopf called it "12 out of 10," February 1991; 4300 Provisional Bomb Wing, Diego Garcia, British-owned territory in the Indian Ocean)

Throughout Operation Desert Storm, Gen. Norman Schwarzkopf provided routine press briefings to cover a range of topics about combat operations. Sometimes, he would show footage of our servicemen taking out a target or would give updates on our progress. On one particular night, he reported on a mission to destroy an ammunition depot, which was one of the strategic goals of the operational plan. During this briefing, Gen. Schwarzkopf told reporters, "If you were to rank an explosion on a scale of one to ten and ten being the biggest, this particular explosion was a 12. The heat signature of this explosion was picked up on satellite and was three times the heat of a space shuttle launch."

It was a B-52 three-ship strike against this particular ammo depot, and I had a front-row seat—well, actually a bottom-row seat based on where the navigators were in the crew compartment. When the crews heard about the news reports, we were high-fiving and laughing it up.

The news sounded pretty cool and the satellite story gave us all our moment-in-the-sun type of publicity, but then there is what Paul Harvey used to refer to as "the rest of the story."

We came in for the briefing and the targeteer took the stage. I had really grown to admire him for his knowledge, expertise, and especially his creative briefings. He said, "Gentlemen, tonight we're going after an ammunition depot." The satellite imagery presented behind him on the screen. The targeteer continued, saying: "We're using a three-ship strike using three types of weapons. We're going to open the lid, stir the pot, and then light the match." What a cool image, right? So, the plan was to use Mk-82s (Pronounced Mark eighty-twos) on the first two ships. The first B-52 would release weapons with no-delay fuses. Those bombs would explode on impact and "open the lid" of the ammo bunkers. The second B-52 would use delayed fuses, which would cause the bomb to penetrate the tops of the weapon bunkers and explode inside the weapon stash or "stir the pot." The third B-52 would then release incendiary cluster bombs. Each cluster bomb would open like a clamshell and release 202 bomblets, which would ignite upon impact or "light the match." The systematic and timed detonation of over 100 500-pound bombs and 10,000 incendiary bomblets would result in a massive explosion.

We took off after we completed our preparation, accomplished two air-refuelings, and entered combat airspace. We were in radio silence and using our forward-looking infrared (FLIR) monitor and our steerable low-light television (STV) monitors to perform station-keeping. Station-keeping is where each B-52 follows the lead aircraft or the one in front of them to keep a predetermined distance and 500 feet altitude separation. More importantly, we watched when the lead aircraft would make a turn and timed for thirty seconds to then make our turn. This would keep everyone in a line, at a safe distance, and separated by altitude.

We were about ten minutes from a 90-degree right turn to head East on a long leg prior to the initial point of the bomb run (IP). I could see clouds coming into view, and the FLIR and STV don't penetrate clouds, so the lead aircraft started to disappear sporadically behind the clouds. Then it vanished from view.

That's why you can never just relax as a navigator during a mission like this. The lead navigator makes all the decisions about when to turn to maintain mission timing, but if you lose lead for some reason, you have to take over. If you turn too early, you cut off that distance, and your aircraft becomes too early; if you turn late, the opposite happens. I would have to make sure we made the turn and flew at the airspeed needed to ensure we stayed as the number two aircraft in the strike.

"Nav-Pilot, you're going to have to make the call for this turn."

"Roger, I got it." I gave the crew a one-minute preturn briefing and told the pilot when to turn. When we rolled out, I checked the timing to the next turn point and asked the pilot to make an airspeed adjustment to ensure that we would be on time at the next turn point.

We then ran all the pre-IP checklists and made sure we would be ready to drop our bombs. For this mission, we were at high altitude (around 34,000 feet). After the third night of the war, the Air Force had won air supremacy and we had very minimal threats at altitude. We approached the IP and turned right onto the bomb run. We were still in the clouds with no sight of lead or number three aircraft. We ran our bomb run checklist and were ready to release.

We faced a new concern. If this were a peacetime training mission, we would have aborted the run due to lack of visibility among the cell (the group of three B-52s). Now, we were going to release our weapons, but we didn't know for certain the location of each aircraft. One was somewhere at an altitude below us, and we were below an aircraft that was somewhere above us. The other important piece of information: We were carrying a mix of weapons and releasing them from different altitudes. Each of us would have a different aim-point based on the ballistics of the weapons. There was a remote possibility that one of us could release on top of the other.

Before we had it all worked out related to all the bad things that could happen, the clouds broke apart and the pilots frantically looked for the other two aircraft. There they were, but not exactly where we expected them. Lead was ahead of us and below us, but off to the left. Three was also ahead of us, but off to the right.

"Nav-Pilot, are we on time?"

"Roger, Pilot, right to the second." Each aircraft was flying to a different point and on its own for timing. All we could do was make sure we were at the right spot and right time for us. I made it sound like it was no big deal, but it was high stress—very high stress.

"10-9-8 … Doors open, 2-1, bombs away." The Bomb Release Interval Computer (BRIC) started to drop the bombs in a series of releases—one after another until all fifty weapons were gone.

Now, remember, the plan was to open the lid, stir the pot, and light the match, right? One, then two, followed by three. Thirty seconds was supposed to span each aircraft's weapon impact. The plan was not supposed to be all weapons falling at one time, but that's exactly what happened. All three aircraft released their weapons at roughly the same time. All 150 bombs struck the target at nearly the same time. Instead of having a systematic series of three rounds of explosions (which by itself would have been pretty impressive), the lid opened, the pot stirred, and the match was lit all at once. It was one of the largest-ever B-52 explosions, so powerful that a satellite reacted to it like it was an enemy's nuclear missile launch. Take that, Saddam!

So, that's how the explosion was a twelve out of ten and we quietly appreciated our moment in the sun.

Just like in combat, civilian life is all about taking the opportunity as it comes. It's kind of like the same thing in preparing for your return to civilian life. Once you leave the military, a somewhat unpredictable process begins in your mind. Chances are almost 100 percent that veterans will encounter challenges in readjusting. Most develop positive coping skills because they naturally follow some of the suggestions in this chapter, their family is naturally more supportive, or they're just better suited.

However, almost one in two veterans will struggle in more significant ways. Though some don't struggle at first, it may happen sometime down the road. So that begs the question: How do you know which group you're in? Are you adjusting well, doing fine until the other shoe drops, or do you struggle immediately? Regardless, you must take a more regimented self-directed effort to reach better outcomes. Even people who are adjusting well can benefit from these practices for improved life satisfaction.

The path to recovery is not straight. It's filled with forwards and backwards, ups and downs, starts and stops. It is, however, a path. Every effort will be met with some kind of resistance. Progress could be slow or nearly invisible. Just like any self-improvement plan, New Year's resolutions, or any other process, it will take discipline and energy. It will take commitment to move from one place to the next.

Chapter 4

CREATING MENTAL STABILITY:

The Science of a Healthy Mind

Plus or minus ten seconds. That was all I had to work with for our time over target. Ten seconds early and the bomb fragments (frag) from the aircraft in front of us would have taken us out. Ten seconds late and we would frag the aircraft behind us. With tolerances like that, why would you risk using more than one bomber? With 50,000 pounds of bombs on board, wouldn't one B-52 be enough? Maybe. It depended on the value, the defense, and the complexity of the target.

Some of our missions used multiple B-52 cells of three to six aircraft attacking a target from multiple axes of attack. Not only were B-52s involved, but we had Wild Weasels (F-4s at the time) searching for surface-to-air radars to attack. In addition, we had airborne radar and command and control assets, and we had other air-to-air fighter support as part of an entire strike package. We employ all of this to kill the enemy and deny them the use of an airfield, fuel storage, communications, vehicles, and munitions.

We never just *barely* destroyed a target or put up *just enough* of a strike package to attack the enemy. We coordinated and planned every asset down to the tiniest detail and to the exact second. We knew to put more than enough assets in the package to win. As an aircrew, we knew every aspect of the target, its defense, and what we would do under a number of circumstances. No one tool was enough, and no one tool worked entirely by itself. Each and every mission took the entire game plan.

In reflecting back on those missions, it's no wonder why we dominated the air war during the first Gulf War. We were so well trained, prepared, and equipped, which made us feel unbelievably confident of success. There is no substitute for preparation and training like we had. I don't care if it's a military mission, a successful Super Bowl run, or living out a successful life after your military service. It is all about knowing what is coming, understanding the tools you have at hand, and having the confidence in using them to succeed.

Many veterans underestimate the challenges of returning home. They're leaving with this unbelievable confidence in themselves and in their abilities to succeed. But the mission is changed when they return. Veterans need new weapons to fight an unknown adversary. Without preparation for what is coming, you can get behind the curve and end up caught in very unfamiliar circumstances. As Franklin D. Roosevelt said, "Men are not prisoners of fate, but only prisoners of their own minds."

Nobody needs to end up on the losing end of this battle. Each of us possesses the tools we require not only to survive but to flourish in this new environment. Our fate is not a prison. We carry within us the mental capacity to solve complex problems and the imagination to envision amazing things. We just need to understand how the mind works and how to utilize every aspect of it to our advantage; not just enough to get by, but to really study the mind, how it works, how the brain works, and how we can use our bodies to maximize our potential. That is the purpose of this chapter.

Franklin Roosevelt's quote is a very interesting reference to the mind acting as a prison. A prison is supposed to be a physical place of constraint. When we talk about our minds, what is it that we're really talking about? We all know what the human brain is, right? It is that mass of gray and white matter in our heads. It contains billions of nerve cells arranged in patterns and groups to coordinate thoughts, emotions, behaviors, movements, and sensations. The brain is the physical place where the mind resides. It is a container in which the electronic impulses that create thought are contained. If we are prisoners of our minds, then we are not in a prison of physical presence. Rather, it means we are prisoners of our collective thoughts and emotions—thoughts and emotions we can change.

In our culture, we sometimes use the words **"brain"** and **"mind"** interchangeably, even though they refer to separate concepts. The brain is an organ, but the mind isn't. The brain is an anatomical, functioning physical thing. With the brain, you coordinate your moves (your activities) and transmit impulses. But you use the mind to think. We can easily point to a leg, a mouth, an ear, or an eye and understand those physical aspects of our brain functions. However, try pointing to the mind. It exists, but you can't touch and feel it. It is our intellect, the composition of our conscious and subconscious thoughts.

If this is slightly confusing, don't worry. You may be surprised to find that no single agreed-upon definition of the mind exists. Psychiatric/mental health and medical professions each have their own functional definitions. But understanding this difference between the brain and the mind and how both work is the one thing you can learn in order to alter the future of your life. The brain and the mind impact our health and wellness. As I'll explain, both are significantly under our control. When it comes to our happiness and satisfaction in life, we can take physical and mental steps that can have a positive impact on our emotional state. Let's unpack each of these at greater length.

The Brain

Without diving into a deep anatomical discussion, the brain is described as a complex organ made up of mostly fat, water, carbohydrates, proteins, and salts. It is a chemical-electrical machine that distributes instructions throughout the body over a network of nerves that lead from the brain across the spinal column. The brain has substance and can be touched and studied.

The human brain, weighing about three pounds, is made up of about 60 percent fat and generates close to twenty-three watts of power (slightly less than a common light bulb) while the person is awake. It requires a steady flow of blood, and an individual may lose consciousness even in a lapse of eight to ten seconds. One hundred billion neurons are present in the brain, and the blood vessels stretch 100,000 miles in length.[20]

It differs from the mind in that it is a physical organ, and it controls aspects of our bodies such as movement, breathing, heart pumping, etc. While it is distinctly different, it is also interconnected with the mind. The mind uses the brain, and the brain responds to the mind. Because of this interconnectedness, we can change the functioning of our brains by

20 https://www.vedantu.com/biology/difference-between-brain-and-mind

the way we think. In addition, we can alter the way we think by how our bodies interact with our brains.

We have control.

"When we're born, our brain is completely malleable and experiencing new things all the time," says Santosh Kesari, MD, PhD, neurologist, neuro-oncologist, and neuroscientist. "We're figuring out positive and negative behaviors, what is good for survival and avoiding consequences that would cause even short-term pain. As we age, our brain learns ways to do things that make us do certain things and behaving accordingly to each context and each stimulus."

Essentially, our brains learn what works and what doesn't early on. This is great on the one hand because it means we don't have to keep relearning positive behaviors. But the downside is that the brain gets used to doing certain things in a certain way so that over time, introducing new behavioral modes becomes challenging.

"Emotionally and cognitively and executively the brain has established a lot of pathways," says Dr. Sanam Hafeez, a licensed clinical psychologist and neuropsychologist. "The more you do something the more ingrained it becomes in neural pathways, much like how a computer that stores the sites you visit—when you log onto your browser, they will pop up because you use them a lot. Change is an upheaval of many things, and the brain has to work to fit it into an existing framework."[21]

These pathways were interrupted when we entered our military careers. Then think about the training, training, and more training. Basic training, advanced training, additional skills training, specialized training, it was all designed to create new neural pathways so that when we needed to respond in combat, we didn't need to think; our neural

21 https://www.nbcnews.com/better/health/how-train-your-brain-accept-change-according-neuroscience-ncna934011

pathways made our movements and reactions happen in fractions of a second. So how do we get our stubborn brains to open up to change? First, we should consider cognitive rehabilitation exercises.

Brain training websites such as Luminosity and BrainHQ help stimulate new neural pathways. "This is like going to the gym for your brain," explains Hafeez. "These sites have visual, spatial, and memory exercises. I say do them three times a week or fifteen minutes a day," she says. "Get into a regimen. You will get frustrated, but that means it's working—just like how your muscles are sore after you take time off from the gym and return. You've been out of touch with this for a while, but the more you do it, the more your memory of how to do it comes back."

By hitting this "mental gym" and working through these mental exercises, you will begin to create a more elastic brain and the groundwork of building new pathways for change.

The Mind

Now that we have discussed the inner workings of the brain, let's shift to a discussion of the mind. The mind makes humans capable of solving complex logical problems. This ability differentiates us from other living beings. Logic makes us understand that things are not as they seem. But our ability to analyze situations makes it possible to develop solutions to problems and leads us toward practical solutions. We may not be able to see with X-ray vision, but we may design instruments to do so. We may not be able to see atoms, but we can design experiments that enable us to know their properties.

Your body responds to the way you think, feel, and act. Stress, anxiety, or being upset causes your body to react in a way that might tell you that something isn't right. Poor emotional health can weaken your immune system, making you more likely to get colds and other infections during emotionally difficult times. Also, when you are stressed, anxious, or upset, you may not take care of your health as well as you should. You may not feel like exercising, eating nutritious food, or taking your prescribed medicine. Abuse of alcohol, tobacco, or other drugs may also be a sign of poor emotional health.

To understand the mind, I'd like to refer to a simplistic model called the Stick Person. Bob Proctor once told me that this simple stick person was the most important thing he learned in order to understand how the mind works. Your conscious mind is your thinking mind. This is where your thoughts take place. The conscious mind can choose thoughts. It receives inputs from our five senses: taste, touch, smell, hearing, sight. The conscious mind can choose what to pay attention to. It can choose specific thoughts, disregard certain images.

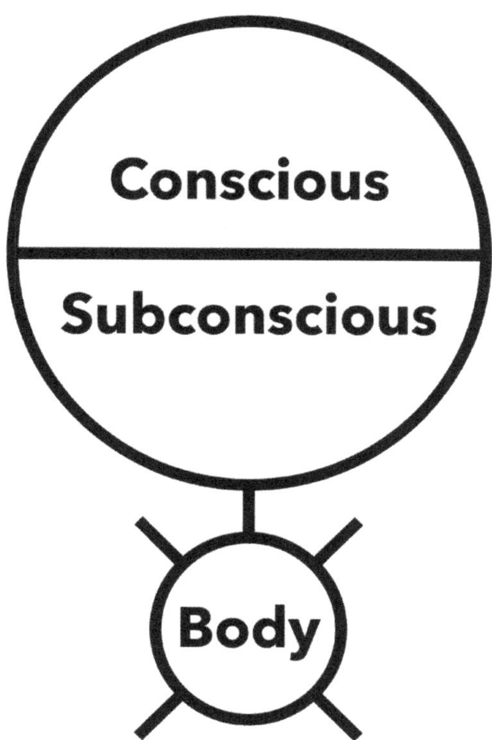

However, the subconscious mind cannot reject any thought or idea that is expressed through the conscious mind; it can only accept what the conscious mind is giving. It cannot differentiate between what's real and imagined. As American author and poet Sidney Madwed describes it, "Our subconscious minds have no sense of humor, play no jokes, and cannot tell the difference between reality and an imagined thought or image. What we continually think about eventually will manifest in our lives."[22]

The conscious is the intellectual part of your personality. It is the thinking and analyzing part of your personality. Your senses are hooked up to your conscious like tiny antennae. They bring in tons of information from the books you read, the people with whom you associate, television, newspapers, friends with whom we talk, and pretty much everything else around you. The conscious can accept or reject any idea, and it can also originate ideas. Ideally, we should question everything we hear or learn and then ask if that information is useful for us—and whether we want to accept or reject it. We rarely do that. In fact, we tend to accept most of what we hear without thinking.

The subconscious is the emotional part of the human personality. Any information that we repetitiously impress upon our conscious enters the subconscious and is then deposited inside the treasury of the subconscious personality. This part of our minds perfectly remembers everything that we have ever encountered. The subconscious cannot reject any idea. It must accept what is impressed upon it. It doesn't matter if we impress thoughts of depression, doom and gloom, or abundance and freedom; it just soaks it in. It then expresses itself through the body in the form of vibrations.[23]

---

22 https://marcallen.com/the-power-of-your-subconscious-mind/

23 https://bobproctorlessons.blogspot.com/2013/03/introducing-stick-person.html

It is the subconscious that makes trauma so dangerous to our psyches. The subconscious doesn't do any filtering. The trauma goes directly to our subconscious without editing, questioning, or understanding. It's just stamped there. I believe this is where nightmares originate for veterans, as the subconscious mind doesn't know how to deal with this unfiltered trauma.

The mind consists of six primary mental faculties of intuition, perception, reason, will, memory, and imagination. Each of these takes place within the brain. "Mind" is often used to refer specifically to the reasoning thought processes. Animals can interpret their environments but not understand them, whereas humans can understand what happens around them even if we don't fully grasp the scientific reasoning behind it. This practice allows each of us to adapt to a situation and make decisions on the fly.

In fact, the subconscious is constantly active, processing and moving you through your day without you even knowing it. It is incredibly powerful and can take on thousands of different tasks and responsibilities, many of which can be performed at the same time. For example, your subconscious blinks your eyes, digests food, regulates blood flow and pressure, and keeps you breathing.[24] But it does so much more. It provides you with new thoughts and ideas and creates novel experiences. A great analogy for the relationship between the conscious and the subconscious is the image of an iceberg. The tip of the iceberg, which resides above water, is like the conscious mind. However, the greater majority of the iceberg is beneath the water. This is like the subconscious mind. Beneath the water lies the majority of the resources and power, just like in the case of your subconscious.

According to Dr. Joseph Murray, author of the worldwide bestseller *The Power of Your Subconscious Mind*, "Within your subconscious

---

24 http://www.power-of-visualization.com/subconscious-mind.html

depths lie infinite wisdom, infinite power, and an infinite supply of all that is necessary." But why is this important for you? As you enlist, train, deploy, and experience the harsh reality of war, your mind shifts. The lens through which you see the world changes as well. That is just what you are aware of. As powerful as your subconscious might be, it acts like a sponge, absorbing experiences, sights, sounds, smells, and all that surrounds you. So, it is only natural that your time in the service extremely impacts and affects you. In some ways, you will grow into a stronger, more dedicated person. Many people will share that they found their true calling and purpose in their service to our country.

Still, others might indicate (or not even know) just how deeply their deployment might have impacted their view of the world. You don't feel your subconscious changing. It just happens, little by little, day by day, moment by moment. The subconscious mind is tremendously powerful. It is like the gas that powers the car. This depth of subconscious influence makes it crucial for us to recognize the importance of putting in the work to create a healthy mind.

One of the most effective ways to do this is through visualization. While deployed, your training likely consisted of some aspect of visualization exercises, focusing on influencing the subconscious to anticipate strategy, situational hazards, and wartime skills. But in returning home, visualization exercises can help you refocus your mind and reconnect to the world around you. Just like you can program your subconscious, you can also reprogram it. Dr. Murray states, "All your experiences, events, conditions, and acts are produced by your subconscious mind in reaction to your thoughts. Remember, it is not the thing believed in, but the belief in your own mind that brings about the results." That means that whatever you think about at the top of your mind eventually makes its way to your subconscious existence.

Your subconscious takes orders from you. Dr. Murray shares that: "Your conscious mind is the captain of the ship. Your subconscious mind takes the orders you give it, based upon what your conscious mind believes and accepts as true. It does not question the orders." Think about that for a second. If you tell yourself you are happy, healthy, and connected, so it will be. And if you constantly express to your mind that you are unhappy, nervous, anxiety ridden, and depressed, so it will be. The point? You have to play your role in influencing your mind in the most productive and meaningful way. If you are experiencing hardship or suffering, you should seek professional help, but supplement it with positive thoughts and inspiration. You will always be a victim of your negative and disempowering beliefs if you continue to allow them to creep in. Ralph Waldo Emerson said, "Man is what he thinks about all day long."

Now that is not to say that you should simply whisper kind remarks and sentiments into your mind. In fact, "positive thinking" without further influence is one of the least effective ways to change your perspective and outlook. Many more empowering options are at your disposal. Your subconscious speaks a different language than your conscious. It is extremely affected by pictures, symbols, and emotions. That is why veterans returning home after deployment are so heavily prejudiced by their service. They are surrounded by very real and powerful experiences, many of which are burned or etched into their subconscious minds. This requires some pretty substantial reprogramming. Visualization is the key to unlock these otherwise closed doors.

Visualizing Happiness

A great deal of literature, writings, studies, and research on visualization techniques and strategies exist. For purposes of our conversation, know that visualization is the language of the subconscious mind. If you hope to recover and reconnect to the world around you, you have to become fluent with your subconscious by speaking the language it understands the best. Otherwise, it is as if you are speaking Spanish to a mind that only understands English. You just won't get anywhere.

Let's focus on exactly how you can use visualization to better impact your life, happiness, and overall success. The good news: Just a few minutes a day can create fantastic results and shift your perspective, emotions, and overall feelings about yourself and the world around you.

In your military training, you have probably used visualization many times without realizing it. You were visualizing as you planned a mission and tried to anticipate what might happen and how you could react to that situation. The more thoroughly you visualized the mission, the better prepared you were and the better the outcome was, at least in theory.

Think about it: Everything we do begins with our thoughts, whether it's something we say, a movement we make; every creation we make as humans exists first as a thought or an image in the imagination. When we anticipate something, we're visualizing. Most of the time, we don't even know we're doing it. Many of our fears are based on us visualizing the negative consequences of something that might or might not happen.

On the positive side, the ability to see things before they happen enables us to pursue our dreams and ultimately achieve them. In fact, the better we visualize the **future we want,** the better our chances to make it happen.

Many psychologists and life coaches recommend mental rehearsal for all sorts of things. It could be work related to handling a difficult employee or preparing to make a presentation to a group of people. It could also be social when getting ready for a date. Athletes at the highest level use visualization to improve their technique, motivation, and drive. Olympic gold medalists have used visualization not just for the sport technique but also to capture the feeling of being awarded the top prize. They picture themselves on the podium on the top step receiving the gold medal.

Bob Proctor uses visualization and acting to help people solidify those feelings. He asked one person to stand up in front of an entire crowd to give an acceptance speech for an Oscar. This was before he ever was nominated for the award. He did what was asked and repeated the experience in his mind over and over. He went back to producing his movie and repeatedly rehearsed his speech. He was nominated for an Oscar and actually won the award. Coincidence? Maybe. But visualization sure is powerful, and high-performing people use it to accomplish their goals.

Here are some basic exercises. Do them in order, moving on to the next one only when you have mastered the first. Take as many days as you like to get really good at each level. There is no rush.[25]

Exercise 1.

Find a photograph and analyze it. Memorize every detail you can. Then simply close your eyes and try to recreate it in your mind. Bring in as much as you can: the colors, the sky, the freckles on the skin—whatever is there in the photograph. Open your eyes to get more detail if you need it. Remember that this is not a test: Do it until you get good at it. The more detail you recreate the better.

Do this exercise over with more than one photo to gain practice.

Exercise 2.

For the second exercise, we'll create something in three dimensions. This time, take up a small object, perhaps your pen or your keys. Again, analyze all the details and memorize them. Take your time.

---

25 https://litemind.com/how-to-develop-visualization-skill/

Now, close your eyes and see the object mentally. The challenge here is to start rotating it. See every detail, but from all angles. If you feel comfortable, begin to bring in some surroundings. Place it on an imaginary table. Shine a few lights on it, and imagine the shadows flickering. Zoom in on the object, and zoom back out.

Exercise 3.

This exercise brings you into the picture. Imagine yourself at an event: a concert, a football game, a fair, or an amusement park. Make it something positive where you would really want to be.

In your mind, create the image with as much detail as you can. Where are you? Is it an outdoor event? Are you in a big crowd? Is it nighttime? How bright are the lights? Imagine yourself as you enjoy the experience. See your friends, your spouse, your children. Keep adding more and more detail to your experience.

Bring in all your senses, one by one. What can you hear? Is the wind rustling? Are people talking in the background? What about the sense of touch? Can you feel what you're sitting or standing on? What about the smell? What colors do you see and what do you smell? Can you imagine eating ice cream and feeling it slide down your throat? I like eating ice-cream sandwiches at football games.

Make this mental movie as strong and vibrant and detailed as you can.

Exercise 4.

Let's make a movie with you as the main character. It can be wherever and whenever you want. It can be now or five years in the future. This movie is about you doing something you really want to do, becoming something you've always wanted to be, making something you've always wanted to make.

Create the scene in as much detail as you can. Bring in the colors, the sounds, the smells. Select your cast. Who is in the movie scene with you? Why are they there? They're proud of what you've done. They can't even believe what you've accomplished, but you have done it. Are they applauding, asking you questions, coming up to congratulate you?

This is your movie to produce.

Now, take the next step and place yourself in the movie and start to experience what your character was experiencing. See the people around you. Feel the feelings of that future you. What's it like?

Then, bring in someone else. Perhaps you could bring in a date and then imagine a dance with him or her. Hold a conversation with them. Imagine them laughing as you tell them a joke. Now, imagine them giving you a hug. What does that feel like?

Detail and Realism

We emphasize detail and realism simply because perfect practice makes perfect.

If I asked you to imagine the execution of your goals—whether it be doing well in a business meeting, or a date, or sports—you probably saw yourself doing it perfectly right away. You win big, you look cool, and everyone falls in love with you. This feels good and can increase motivation, but, to put it bluntly, it's mostly a waste of time.

Realism is the most important consideration in visualization. Soldiers train in almost exactly the same gear and the same environment they will experience in combat. We used realistic flight simulators, and special ops practiced on models of the targeted facility. No one gets really good just by playing shooting games on the computer or paintball. The more realistic the training, the better the outcome. The more times you practice, the more real the outcome becomes.

You need to bring in realism. When you begin visualizing properly, your heart will be beating fast, you might feel anxious or excited, and you may even feel some fear. Any improvements you make there would also begin to carry over into the real world.

And all this, while you're sitting on the couch!

Applying Visualization to Your Goals

Now, what if we're not dealing with a physical skill? What if you had set a goal for something like money, a new career, or a holiday?

Visualization applies in much the same way. Consider these tips for applying it to your goals:

1. **Focus on the positive.** A common mistake is focusing on the opposite of what you want. When people want to lose weight, they post pictures of their fat bellies all over their room, thinking that is motivating them. But that is the wrong way: By focusing on their fat, they are keeping the fat there. They should visualize the stomach they want.
2. **Have it, don't want it.** Think of something you really, really want. Now, do you have it? Probably not. Most often, wanting is the opposite of having. So, when you visualize, don't think about wanting something, see yourself as already having it.
3. **Be consistent.** You have to really work hard on this. Your mind is a muscle, just like your body. The top bodybuilders didn't get to their positions by working out for two minutes a day. They worked hard for it. Make your goal your burning obsession, a passion, and purpose in life.
4. **Be specific.** Most people have vague goals. They vaguely want to be rich, or they want to travel somewhere nice. Where? Oh,

> never thought about it much. It's like getting into a car with a vague goal of wanting to buy … something. Not going to happen, right? You want to have a specific goal: I'm going out to the supermarket to buy myself some shampoo and a toothbrush. It is the same with your goals. Set it in as much detail as you can: a specific amount of money, a specific outcome from a meeting, whatever it is.

Remember, visualization is a very powerful tool for helping you achieve your goals.

Understanding (then Avoiding) Our Chemistry[26]

For all we know about how to positively impact our subconscious, we are readily aware of many pitfalls that can impact it too. It is just as important to avoid these as you navigate your return from service and constant desire to reconnect with the world around you. We are pre-wired to experience bliss and enjoy happiness. But the world shakes us, turns us, and throws us around. In doing so, it impacts our ability to be happy. It cuts deep into our subconscious existence and leaves us feeling bumped and bruised. Fundamentally, all animals seek pleasure and work to avoid pain. And as we produce many neurochemicals, we seemingly feel pretty good. But it is just as important to be aware and guard against the very real and significant threats that attack our happiness and existence.

There is a reason why we might wake up feeling blah or sad. It isn't a coincidence. It is a result of our minds and bodies working against us, not with us. It is common to have a day here and there where you just

26 https://www.psychologytoday.com/us/blog/the-mindful-self-express/201411/10-scientific-reasons-you-re-feeling-depressed

cannot move in the right direction. But if you find yourself having more bad days than good, then analyze and understand exactly why that's so. Let's look at some reasons why many people feel out of sorts:

1. **Brain Chemicals.** This should come as no surprise. Brain chemicals are sensitive to a whole host of influencers, including stress and anxiety. Diet, exercise, and lifestyle choices also impact brain chemicals considerably.
2. **Weather.** Ever walk outside and immediately feel unhappy? Well, that's because it is probably raining or overcast. Sunshine promotes the release of neurochemicals. A study by US psychology researcher Matthew Keller and colleagues studied hundreds of people and found that during the spring, people's moods improved as they did more outdoors. In fact, some of us might even suffer from seasonal affective disorder, where winter months cause depression and changes in sleep and motivation[27].
3. **Vitamin D Depletion.** Vitamin D deficiency has been statistically linked to depression. In a large Dutch study by Witte J. Hoogendijk and colleagues (2008) of over 1,200 people aged sixty-five and older, levels of vitamin D were 14 percent lower in people with minor depression or major depressive disorder when compared to those not showing depressed mood.
4. **Hormones.** Hormones influence many bodily functions, like mood, sexual ability, and metabolism. They can fluctuate from time to time, and certain hormones can impact your entire mood or very specific portions of it.
5. **Expectations.** Set realistic expectations. If you expect the best meal you've ever had and only get a pretty good one, you might

27 https://theconversation.com/here-comes-the-sun-how-the-weather-affects-our-mood-19183

find yourself disappointed. The same is true with friendships, relationships, and outlook on life. Manage your expectations to be realistic, especially when returning home after deployment.

6. **Stress.** This can include current situations or past experiences. Stress attacks your happiness and is one of the greatest threats to your ability to live a meaningful life. Focus on the controllables, and don't let small things derail your joy.
7. **Perspective.** As mentioned, your perspective or life outlook can readily impact your chemistry. Keep telling your mind you are sad, and you will be sad. But the converse is also true. Research studies by University of Michigan psychologist Susan Nolen-Hoeksema and colleagues show that sitting around thinking about your negative mood or negative events just makes everything worse!
8. **Loneliness.** We all need love and support. Surround yourself with people who care for you and love you. Love is an essential human function, and it makes it increasingly more difficult to be sad when people who care about your best interests surround you. We are wired to be part of a social group, and isolation further disconnects us from all the positive occurring in the world around us.[28]

A large number of reasons may be behind why you feel down and out. But there is good news: You can take more avenues and steps to recapture your happiness and vigor for life. Your mind is a tremendously robust and complicated vessel. Within it lives your subconscious, which can literally move mountains for you. As a veteran, very likely your sub-

28 https://www.psychologytoday.com/blog/the-mindful-self-express/201411/ten-scientific-reasons-why-you-re-feeling-depressed

conscious has been programmed for a flight-or-fight response and certainly impacted by your stressful and difficult experiences. But as you return home and re-engage with the world around you and the people you love, do everything you can to reprogram your mind to position you best for success.

The next section of this chapter will help you better understand how your military training and deployment shape your perspective on the world. Hopefully, once you further understand your perspective you can then work to change it. Earl Nightingale said, "Whatever we plant in our subconscious mind and nourish with repetition and emotion will one day become a reality." Together, we will work to help you build a more meaningful, happy reality.

Transforming the Mind and Body

Until you enrolled in the armed forces, your mind worked in a very specific way. It was generally the product of all that happened around you, and most people had a relatively mild and easy existence. But when you joined, the military took specific, conscious actions to shift the way you started to think as well as the way your mind reacted to certain situations.

Military education and training offer its personnel a complete transformation. The social skills, tools, and behaviors you were used to and called "the norm" as a civilian will slowly be replaced with a special type of training focused on a number of different skill sets you might have never even considered.

Military education begins with a full mental and physical examination. The powers that be must qualify you to serve our country. First, they ensure that you are physically capable of enduring the hardships of service; then they determine if you are mentally healthy to bear the extreme toll service can take on your mind. Assuming you make it past this rigorous testing, you can then begin to complete your primary training. This training is often referred to as recruit training. Recruit training attempts to teach the basic information and training in techniques necessary to help you be an effective service member.

After completing recruit training, you might then transition into a more specialized and specific training depending on your area of expertise or interest. It could range from technology to combat to intelligence. This is often referred to as advanced training; a tremendous number of potential paths from which to choose exist. In fact, at times the path will choose you, as the government might decide to use your experience and training prior to entering service to find the right specialization for you. Larger countries like the United States have a number of different military academies, which act like collegiate universities and offer further information and training to recruits. No matter the case, the mind and body shift begins with extensive training.

Simultaneous with this training, the government is also focusing on the notion of resocialization, which is the process of inducting a civilian into the military. It is often considered a reprogramming of sorts, so a person can operate in an environment other than what they are accustomed to. However, this also might change the individual's fundamental, basic concept of self and the world around him or her. This is an extremely process-oriented task, and a tremendous amount of time and effort has gone into the most optimal way to accomplish this goal.

But the alternative is not always as easy. Resocializing from a life of combat to a life of a civilian is much harder than the other way around. This is often based on the difficulties a soldier has experienced in the military. It isn't particularly easy to "unring" the bell. A leading expert in military training methods, Lt. Col. (Ret.) Dave Grossman gives four types of training techniques used[29]:

- Brutalization
- Classical conditioning
- Operant conditioning
- Role modeling

According to Grossman, these techniques aim to break down barriers to embracing a new set of norms and way of life (brutalization); to condition trainees to pair killing with something more enjoyable and pleasurable (classical conditioning); to repeat the stimulus-response reaction to develop a reflex (operant conditioning); and finally, to use a "role model" of a superior to provide action by example. While leaders effectively train their soldiers to accomplish the goal of battle preparedness, these techniques increase psychological trauma experienced in veterans post-combat. On Military1.com, writer Rachel Engel outlines nine ways the military changes you. These include the following:[30]

1. **It instills a sense of purpose.** In the military, you have a goal at all times. You are striving to reach the next level, to become a better leader, to get things right every single time. It's not just about you; it's about the team, the unit, the mission.
2. **It forces you to look at the bigger picture.** Someone with previously little interest in foreign affairs learns quickly that in the

29 https://en.wikipedia.org/wiki/Military_education_and_training#cite_note-1
30 https://www.military1.com/military-lifestyle/article/1637637014-9-ways-the-military-changes-you/

military, you need to have at least a basic understanding of world events. That's because when a global crisis happens, it will often affect the military. Serving your country means becoming aware of our place in the world.

3. **It provides a sense of appreciation for what we have.** The ability to travel is one of the biggest perks of serving. Who else can say their job allows them to live on nearly every continent? However, no matter how amazing living overseas can be, when your plane touches down in the United States after a deployment or an OCONUS assignment, nearly every service member will say, "There's no place like home."
4. **It creates pride in your work.** A job in the military isn't "just" a job—it's part of a mission that's part of a larger mission that's part of an even larger mission. An Air Force mechanic stationed in New Mexico is making a difference halfway around the world in Qatar by meticulously performing his task to the best of his ability, knowing that mistakes he makes could cost lives.
5. **It teaches cooperation with those different from you.** In a war zone, troops often work with coalition forces, or other units from the US, particularly on bases in the region. Cultural experiences, viewpoints, and ideas can clash, creating a potentially difficult work situation. Troops don't have time for that. The job has to be done, the mission is on the line, and you must compromise and complete it. Period.
6. **It shows you how to make the most out of a difficult situation.** The military lifestyle is rough. No matter how much you enjoy your job, you're always having to say "goodbye" to loved ones and "hello" to long days, stressful situations, and a lack of home comforts. Rising above the hard times, the moments when

the deployment seems like it will never end is a critical skill for service members.

7. **It teaches adaptability.** Very few jobs are as prone to spur-of-the-moment changes and diversity as military jobs. Moving at the drop of the hat, missing major milestones, going with the flow when higher-ups completely change the way things are done—not easy to deal with, and service members do it daily. Adapt and overcome.
8. **It proves that everything is temporary.** Don't like where you're living? Give it a year or two and you'll get orders. Over this deployment? Hang on a few more months, and you can go home. Not a huge fan of your boss? Chances are he'll get orders soon, too.
9. **It helps perfect the art of the goodbye.** Goodbye to your loved ones before boot camp. Goodbye to your buddies from basic. Goodbye to your wife before a deployment. Goodbye to a brother who gave the ultimate sacrifice. Goodbye to your children before another deployment. Goodbye to amazing friends during a Permanent Change of Station (PCS). Goodbyes are a part of life, and nowhere is that more evident than in the military.

Just think about each of these changes for a few minutes. Any one of these would completely change your outlook on life and your relationship with the world around you. Now combine each one and you can likely imagine just how reprogrammed any one serviceman or woman may be. My point in sharing these with you is to demonstrate the substantial amount of reprogramming you undergo after you enlist. That begs the question: Why are military boot camps so intense?[31] The

31 http://www.slate.com/blogs/quora/2013/03/05/why_is_boot_camp_so_intense.html

answers vary, but here is one of most impactful, as outlined on a blog posted on Slate.com:

Jon Davis, Marine sergeant, Iraq vet, weapons instructor: "You have to train eighteen-year-olds to run to the sound of gunfire and perform under fire and the threat of death. This act defies all logic, goes against all human instinct, and takes one of the most intensive acts of psychological reprogramming to overcome."

As you can imagine, boot camps and training are so important because these young men and women are just months—if not weeks—away from being involved in modern warfare. They have no time for hesitation, on-the-job training, or mistakes. If they make a mistake, they or their fellow servicemen could die. Our government works to train warriors, a practice that dates back to the beginning of time. Sometimes we have no choice but to fight for survival. And survival calls for training. Even with the advent of drones, stealth warfare, and high-tech weaponry, there will still be a need for the frontline cavalry equipped with guns in hand to fight the good fight. Our nation needs this, and the safety of us in our homes often relies upon this.

Our training reflects this need. The psychological and physical preparedness is a mirror of the battlefield. According to Engel, "That is why boot camp has evolved to become such a potent tool in today's military machine." So, we can only assume that boot camps are designed to reprogram how people act and react. Sadly, this calls for the removal of some fashion of the human element. Imagine the risk to us all if our nation's servicemen run onto the battlefield thinking about their children and parents. Our training programs are designed to remove this human element and individuality and replace it with a common goal: to protect our country.

Think of the simple yet representative act of cutting your hair. Each and every Marine is required to cut his hair and shave his head. Why?

Because everyone is the same in boot camp. Same look. Same feel. Same person with the same goal. Each and every part of the training process is purposeful. Each drill or decision is part of a larger reprogramming process that occurs at the beginning of your enlistment. A large number of habits and behaviors have to be unlearned; and it isn't easy to reprogram the mind. That is why boot camp seems like an unequivocal assault on your mind and sense of uniqueness. The military doesn't want unique. We want trained killers with the physical and mental prowess to get the job done, even in the most horrible of circumstances. Some of the most powerful ways to do this include endurance training, isolation from the outside world, yelling to stimulate stress, and much more.

It isn't a pretty process, but it is a necessary mindset. Transforming the mind and body from a lifestyle of happiness and just existing to addressing the fear of the battlefield and surviving isn't the most palatable of narratives. However, it is a story that needs to be told—for those that serve and for their family members. People must have insight into, and a detailed understanding of, the great lengths the military goes to reprogram. In part, that is why it is so remarkably difficult to return home and just reconnect. Combine the horrors of warfare with this training and it is completely realistic that people will change. But they are not lost forever. Just as the mind can be reprogrammed for battle, it can also be retrained for love and happiness in civilian life. But that reprogramming takes time and effort. The power of the mind is the topic of the final section of this chapter.

Transitions: The Invisible Power of the Mind

We exist in a powerful sense of paradigms, which are how we view and relate to the world around us. Those paradigms quickly shift as we enlist in the military. But they can also return to their original positions. They drive our habitual behavior and immediate reaction to everything we see and hear. In Maxwell Maltz's book *Psycho-Cybernetics*, he argues that the most important discovery in psychology in the last century is that of "self-image," the image we hold in our minds, which holds the power to drive our everyday behaviors, beliefs, and outcomes. That image changes drastically through the intensive training that occurs prior to deployment.

As vets transition back into the real world after their service, they have to shift one paradigm for another. After living in a world of conflict and constant struggle, they avoid shifting back to what should be a much less stressful environment. But their minds remain back in service. This section should help vets understand the work they will need to do to shift back to some semblance of normality and the ability to connect. Bob Proctor says it best:[32]

Paradigms—what are they? Is it a buzzword for the information age? It very well may be, but it's one you need to seriously consider. Because if you're like most people, paradigms are controlling every move you make. Paradigms are a multitude of habits that guide every move you make. They affect the way you eat, the way you walk, even the way you talk. They govern your communication, your work habits, your successes, and your failures.

For the most part, your paradigms didn't originate with you. They're the accumulated inheritance of other people's habits, opinions, and belief systems. Yet they remain the guiding force in YOUR life. Negative and faulty paradigms are why ninety-some percent of the population keeps getting the same results, year in and year out.

A walking path through a forest is very similar to a paradigm. Depending on how long it's been used, the path can be well worn and

---

32 http://www.proctorgallagherinstitute.com/1974/understanding-the-power-of-paradigms

deep and easy to walk on. It's very hard to walk through a forest, for example, near a path and stay off it. Why make it harder? That's why people stay within their own well-worn paradigms. If there's a path already, why would you try to make a new path? In this analogy, it could be that the existing path takes an extra hour and passes by a waterfall that you can't see.

What about you? Is success slipping through your fingers? Do you feel like you're doing all the right things to achieve your goals and get to where you want to be in life, but still can't seem to get there? Do you see people with more money, more success, more happiness than you have and think, *'What am I doing wrong?'* I can tell you right now that the problem isn't you. It's your paradigms. If you want to change your results—really change them, forever—shifting your paradigms is the only way to do it. When that shift happens, *everything* becomes different ... just like THAT.

In order to replace an old paradigm that doesn't serve you, you must lay a new paradigm over that old one, ensuring that it's sealed from "leaking through" again. When you understand how to lay this new path, so to speak, you will expose yourself to a brand-new world of power, possibility, and promise. *Remember: there will be no permanent change in your life until the paradigm has been changed.* Choose one or two limiting ideas that are part of your paradigm and replace them with ideas that represent freedom to you. Consciously keep those new thoughts in your head, and act as if those thoughts are already embedded in the foundation of your life. Before you know it, your life will begin to change—dramatically!

We should all consider this attitude when discussing our own personal paradigms. Thomas S. Kuhn introduced the concept of paradigms in his book *The Structure of Scientific Revolutions.* He says: "A paradigm is a set of rules, mindsets, regulations, or procedures that create boundaries or limitations and tell you how to conduct your behavior (make your choices) within those boundaries or limitations in order to meet with success. A paradigm is a filter through which we perceive, interpret, and understand our reality." The reality? Our view of the world is somewhat of a mirror of what we are and who we are. We digest information and then interpret a version of that content.

No doubt, our military service has forever changed our lives. Many of those changes are great for helping us succeed; however, many of us hang on to paradigms, which were either created for us in our training or by us in our experiences. Whichever method of instilling these paradigms, they have been locked into our subconscious minds as true.

When I review the regrets of my life or time in service, I see images or have memories that are sometimes very bitter. For example, after we attacked our first target on the third night of the war, I looked up to see indicators that two 1,000-pound bombs were hung up on the racks in the belly of our B-52. We couldn't continue to carry these weapons because we didn't know their status. No way could we aerial refuel if even a remote possibility existed that they were unsafe. Were they safe or just hanging by a small thread? Had they become armed, or was the pin still lodged in the nose of the bomb? We had to jettison the bombs, so we ran the checklist and successfully released the hung weapons. Where? I have no idea. I know they didn't explode because there was no sign of an explosion.

Whenever I think of those two bombs, I'm disappointed in myself. I hated having to leave them for others on the ground knowing that they could have been unintentionally killed. I hope that the bombs were never used to harm any civilians or our own men and women. Thinking too long on this still creates a very strong discomfort; that's the case even though my rational mind tells me that I had nothing to do with the bombs hanging or that I did what was required to ensure the safety of my crew and others.

These are difficult thoughts and memories, but we have to delete them from our minds. These experiences have formed us, but they are useless to us now because we can do nothing about them and they no longer serve a beneficial purpose. They serve like scars on the face of one of Dr. Maltz's plastic surgery patients. It becomes all we see when we look in the mirror of our self-image. We need less of those thoughts and more of the thoughts of who we want to become. We need to stop ruminating on the negative experiences that form this negative self-image and to spend our time creating a better self-image.

For me, I know it is wasted energy; I described the memory above for the benefit of this book, but in truth, I rarely consider the memory. I've moved on and forgiven myself (at least I've tried). Many of these memories may never be completely erased; however, the key is to fight the good fight and diminish the role these memories play in our daily lives and our self-image and to constantly work at increasing our thoughts and desires about what we want in life. But how do we do that? Endless literature, teachers, resources, and guides claim to help you shift your mindset. In the end, shifting paradigms starts with you. Author Ryan Voigt shares his six tips for improving your self-esteem:[33]

1. **Maximize the positive and minimize the negative.** Focus on your abilities more than your limitations. Everyone has both abilities and limitations. This is not to say that you don't acknowledge that you have a disability, but rather, by focusing

33 Who Me? Self-Esteem for People with Disabilities, *Ryan J. Voigt, MA, UW-Eau Claire Counseling Services*

on and developing your abilities you can feel good about all the things you can do.

2. **Avoid unrealistic comparisons**. Don't get caught up in comparing apples to oranges. Everyone has both strengths and limitations. A person with a locomotor disability may not be able to compete in Olympic ice hockey, but he or she can compete in Paralympic Sledge hockey.
3. **Set realistic goals for yourself.** Since everyone has limitations, it is not fair to expect yourself to be able to do something unrealistic. This may mean allowing yourself to take the extra time needed to read the material and rewarding yourself for persevering. It may not be realistic to expect yourself to read something in the same amount of time as someone without a reading disability.
4. **Do not over-generalize.** If there is something that you cannot do as a result of your disability, it is not fair to conclude that you are an overall failure. There are many things that you can do. Don't tie all of your self-worth to any one attribute or event. Just because you might be a lousy cook does not mean that you are a lousy person in general.
5. **Avoid getting caught using "should" statements.** For example, a student with ADHD says, "I should be able to finish this exam in 50 minutes like everyone else in the class." This is an example of a "should" statement that may not be accurate. Accommodations like extra time on tests are an important tool to create equal opportunities for students to show what they know.
6. **Appreciate yourself—all of yourself**. This means appreciating your disability too. There may be times when you believe that it is more annoying than appreciable but focus on the positive

aspects of your disability. One way to do this is making a list of your strengths including how your disability, or your methods of coping with it, can be an asset.

To deepen the conversation further, I'd like to add my own tip as well:

7. **Don't always be the realist.** When my wife and I discuss our thinking on many topics, I am usually the optimistic voice in the conversation. She calls herself the realist (I call her the pessimist, but that's for a different time). What is realistic and what is optimistic in looking at the future? It's a matter of perspective. In this book, we're trying to create a positive image, so we don't need the dose of the "realist."

These tips can act as reminders about how we can work to shift our paradigms. Our minds are extraordinarily powerful. While the training and boot camps might turn us into trained killers, we have to retrain and reprogram our minds back to being trained civilians. That singular act is not always easy. But it is necessary to readapt and reacquaint yourself and your life with the norms of civilian living. The invisible power of the mind can help you accomplish just that. As you transition from service to civilian, you have to work to develop your mental stability. It takes time, energy, patience, and tremendous effort. But you can do that. This chapter shows you at least a little bit of how.

Chapter 5

FINDING PHYSICAL WELL-BEING:

Adjusting to a New Type of Challenge

As veterans return home and adjust to a new lifestyle, they typically face a series of challenges and obstacles to reentry. Most will tell you that they find their challenges to be predominantly based on readjusting their mind to a calmer and more collected sense of life; but focusing on the mind alone will not do the trick. In fact, any veteran's physical health will almost certainly play a tremendous role in their ability to reconnect and readapt to the world around them. Unwittingly, most servicemen and women find themselves constantly testing the limits of their minds and bodies while serving our country. They might not even realize it, but the physical tasks and responsibilities of service support a strong mind and healthy lifestyle. They then return home and cannot find the same outlets for their energy.

Think about it for a second. Most people in the Army will tell you their day rarely consists of sitting around and doing very little. They are always moving, whether it be on long hikes with equipment strapped to their backs for a mission or just training on the base to ensure that their bodies remain in peak physical condition. A strong body means a strong mind, and a strong mind means a strong body. They are not mutually independent and absolutely rely on one another.

Why is that? To start, it is because of how the brain interacts with the body. The brain works through a series of chemical and electrical impulses. It has a fountain of self-produced neurochemicals that turn the pursuits and struggles of life into pleasure and make us feel happy when we achieve them. While our body produces hundreds of neurochemicals, scientists have only identified a fraction of them. To that end, whether they know it or not, the constant movement and exercise most veterans experienced while enlisted helped to develop their brains and support their happiness. They then return home and search for the same level of structure in their daily routine but often fall seemingly short. That is the issue here. Once you remove the detailed structure, many veterans find that they fall short of accomplishing those pursuits that gave them so much purpose during their service to our country. So, to better understand why happiness is often lost when returning home, you must have at least a surface-level understanding of how the brain stays happy.

It's not to say that our time in service is always bliss filled. Training and exercise are certainly not a constant dream. Part of the challenge returning vets face is the desire to reject the structure that was part of the new normal of military duty. However, this structure played an important part in a process that became a part of who we were during our service. Suddenly eliminating that structure and the neurochemicals associated with those activities set up changes in our minds and bodies for which we are unprepared. But knowledge of these processes is the key to surviving the transition.

The Happy Brain[34]

Seven molecules are linked to happiness, according to scientists. They are the Neurochemicals of Happiness.

1. **Endocannabinoids: "The Bliss Molecule"**
   Endocannabinoids are self-produced cannabis that work on receptors of the cannabinoid system. A study at the University of Arizona, published in April 2012, argues that endocannabinoids are, most likely, the cause for runner's high. The study reveals that humans and dogs show significantly increased endocannabinoids following sustained running.
2. **Dopamine: "The Reward Molecule"**
   Dopamine is responsible for reward-driven behavior and pleasure seeking. Every type of reward-seeking behavior that has been studied increases the level of dopamine transmission in the brain. If you want to get a hit of dopamine, set a goal and achieve it. Some of the best ways to naturally create more dopamine include: laughing out loud, achieving small but realistic goals, setting targets across the board (work, personal, professional), kissing or showing affection, and things that involve touch, like petting your dog or getting a massage.
3. **Oxytocin: "The Bonding Molecule"**
   The hormone oxytocin is directly linked to human bonding and increasing trust and loyalty. In some studies, high levels of oxy-

34 https://www.psychologytoday.com/us/blog/the-athletes-way/201211/the-neurochemicals-happiness

tocin have been correlated with romantic attachment. Some studies show that if a couple is separated for a long time, the lack of physical contact reduces oxytocin and drives the feeling of longing to bond with that person again. You can increase your oxytocin through skin-to-skin contact, affection, lovemaking, and intimacy.

In a cyberworld, where we are often "alone together" on our digital devices, it is more important than ever to maintain face-to-face intimate human bonds and "tribal" connections within our communities. Working out at a gym, in a group environment, or having a jogging buddy is a great way to sustain these human bonds and release oxytocin.

4. **Endorphin: "The Pain-Killing Molecule"**

   The name "endorphin" translates into "self-produced morphine." Endorphins resemble opiates in their chemical structure and have analgesic properties. Endorphins are produced by the pituitary gland and the hypothalamus during strenuous physical exertion, sexual intercourse, and orgasm. Make these pursuits a part of your regular life to keep the endorphins pumping. Endorphins are linked to the "feeling no pain" aspect of aerobic exercise and are produced in larger quantities during high-intensity "anaerobic'" cardio and strength training. You can naturally increase your endorphin levels by exercising at least thirty minutes per day, sweating more through running, steaming, or walking, and playing competitive sports with your friends.

5. **GABA: "The Antianxiety Molecule"**

   GABA is an inhibitory molecule that slows down the firing of neurons and creates a sense of calm. You can increase GABA naturally by practicing yoga, meditation, or "The Relaxation

Response." A study from the *Journal of Alternative and Complementary Medicine* found a 27 percent increase in GABA levels among yoga practitioners after a sixty-minute yoga session when compared to participants who read a book for sixty minutes. The study suggests yoga might increase GABA levels naturally.

6. **Serotonin: "The Confidence Molecule"**

   Serotonin plays so many roles in our bodies that it is really tough to tag it. For the sake of practical application, scientists call it "The Confidence Molecule." Serotonin allows people to put themselves in situations that will bolster self-esteem, increase feelings of worthiness, and create a sense of belonging. To increase serotonin, challenge yourself regularly and pursue things that reinforce a sense of purpose, meaning, and accomplishment. Being able to say, "I did it!" will produce a feedback loop that will reinforce behaviors that build self-esteem, make you less insecure, and create an upward spiral of more and more serotonin. Some ways to increase your serotonin include being outside in the sunlight, exercising, eating carbohydrate-rich (and even spicy) food, and enjoying personal connection and touch.

7. **Adrenaline: "The Energy Molecule"**

   Adrenaline, technically known as epinephrine, plays a large role in the fight-or-flight mechanism. The release of epinephrine is exhilarating and creates an energy surge. Adrenaline causes an increase in heart rate and blood pressure and works by causing less important blood vessels to constrict and increasing blood flow to larger muscles. An EpiPen is a shot of epinephrine used to treat acute allergic reactions.

   An "adrenaline rush" happens in times of distress or facing fearful situations. Doing things that terrify you or being thrust into a

> situation that feels dangerous can trigger it. An adrenaline surge makes you feel very alive. It can be an antidote to boredom, malaise, and stagnation. Taking risks and doing scary things that force you out of your comfort zone are key to maximizing your human potential. However, people often act recklessly to get an adrenaline rush. If you're an "adrenaline junkie," try to balance potentially harmful novelty-seeking by focusing on behaviors that will release other feel-good neurochemicals on this list.[35]

No pharmaceuticals, legal or illicit, prescribed or over the counter, are absent of negative side effects. Some side effects are debilitating, and some are catastrophic. There is a place for pharmacologic treatments under professional treatment; however, this section's aim is to point out that these neurochemicals are naturally produced and, in many cases, a simple increase in activity can help generate the production of the exact healthy neurochemicals the doctor would have ordered.

There is no one-size-fits-all prescriptive when creating a neurochemical balance that correlates to a sense of happiness. Look at the seven neurochemicals as a rudimentary checklist to take inventory of your daily habits and to keep your life balanced. By focusing on lifestyle choices that secrete each of these neurochemicals, you will increase your odds of happiness across the board.

Each of these molecules plays a pivotal role in making you feel happy. As you naturally increase each of them, you feel better and avoid the depression, stress, anxiety, and unhappiness that often come with readjusting to life after service. So, it is important to take the natural

35 https://www.psychologytoday.com/blog/the-athletes-way/201211/the-neurochemicals-happiness

steps available to introduce great levels of happy molecules in your life. Doing exactly that is the topic of the rest of this chapter.

Sleep: The Key to Well-Being

When it comes to your overall mind-body health, sleep rises above all else as the single most important area of focus. Think about the role sleep plays in your life. Ever have a headache and decide to take a nap? You probably felt better afterward. Ever find yourself really hungry? A quick nap probably resolved the issue. What about just feeling exhausted from the day? Nothing a good night's sleep couldn't cure. Frustrated by the day and obstacles you faced? Sleep likely left you feeling recharged and gave you the reset you needed.

Many times, sleep is the enemy in military service. Try flying a nineteen-hour long combat mission with times of extreme stress and then being required to maintain alertness to conduct an aerial refueling needed to make it home. Or in the case of a pilot, try being prepared to land a plane at the end of a mission like that. Chances are your sleep cycle changed multiple times in a month, but keeping alert can mean the difference between life and death. We lost three members of a fellow B-52 crew when they lost control of their aircraft with cascading technical problems combined with a lack of proper sleep.

Military service demanded our ability to put off sleep and to perform unbelievable tasks with very little rest. And sleep didn't always come in the form of a comfortable bed; rather, it was wherever and whenever you could find it. It wasn't always over the course of a complete eight-hour sleep cycle. One time, as a navigator on a B-52 mission, the pilot asked me to sit in his seat while he took a nap. This wasn't all that uncommon due to the length of the missions and the fact that we were over the middle of the Indian Ocean. When I left my seat, I noticed the radar navigator sleeping. When I climbed the ladder to the pilot's cabin, I noticed that the gunner and the EW (electronic warfare officer) were sleeping. I passed by the pilot as he sprawled out on the deck for some needed shut-eye. I sat down and knew all I had to do was make minor adjustments to one or two throttles to "station-keep" behind the two B-52s in front of me. After about half an hour, I looked over to see that the copilot had dozed off too. I was the only one awake and flying an eight-engine B-52 over the Indian Ocean. I was proud to enable the crew to have the luxury of sleep. We had been changing our sleep cycle with alternating day/night missions, and everyone was behind the sleep curve. Please don't tell anybody we did that.

It is common to be tired during your time in service to this country. Remember, you're not working a nine-to-five job. You are in constant threat and dealing with emergency after emergency, which doesn't lend to a relaxing eight hours of consecutive sleep. In fact, you probably have to steal your sleep hours when you can. You get used to being tired and functioning, probably not even recognizing the true impact sleep deprivation can have on you.

Once you return home, you likely have a limited number of excuses about why you cannot sleep. But even then, you simply can't find yourself getting eight hours. Your body is reprogrammed and cannot relax or shut down for the evening. Often then, nightmares, sweats, or other challenges interrupt sleep.

For me, it happened so fast. The nightmares started from out of nowhere about six months after I returned home. They weren't Friday the 13th type nightmares. They were very real, very detailed, and in living color. Intense violence filled these dreams. Though I was in the Air Force, my nightmares included hand-to-hand combat where I would end up killing someone in an extremely gory way. Sometimes I would get shot in the head while I was hiding behind a barrier. I could feel the blood running down my face. But, I also experienced what our enemies might have known when we flew over, seeing our bombs exploding and a nuclear bomb detonating nearby. My reactions whilst asleep would frighten my wife, whether physical or vocal. It was a scary time.

After about six months, the nightmares ended, and my life returned to normal. As suddenly as they appeared, they stopped. Years passed without any struggles except for severe irritability. Then it happened again after 9/11 and an increase in work-related stress. No warning, no symptoms, just nightmares—pretty much the same as the first time, only this time they didn't go away. As a result, I really didn't want to go to sleep because I knew what was going to happen in a couple of hours.

So, I'd have a couple of drinks before bed. That seemed to help a little and if a little helps a little, then a lot could help a lot, right? And, when you're mixing your own drinks, who's to say how much is the right amount? Before you know it, you need the alcohol to get to sleep. For some, it's probably more than alcohol. I was fortunate though and realized that the alcohol wasn't really helping me sleep. It was making matters worse.

The problem was always my irritability and losing my cool. My wife had to walk on eggshells for fear of triggering my temper. The kids had the same fear. The biggest regret of my life is not seeking help sooner. I had become the father I never wanted to be and the husband I'd be embarrassed of because of this constant irritability. Because of the sleep deprivation and the increasing irritability, I finally decided to seek help from the VA.

When I went to the VA, they prioritized me getting sleep as my first important task. My psychiatrist once told me that if they could just get veterans to sleep well, the majority of PTSD symptoms would go away.

Human beings are designed to operate with a certain amount of sleep. If that level is not maintained over a long time, the mind and body will begin to deteriorate. While some believe sleep is overrated, the importance is so well defined that it cannot be ignored.

The National Heart, Lung, and Blood Institute states: "Sleep plays a vital role in good health and well-being throughout your life. Getting enough quality sleep at the right times can help protect your mental health, physical health, quality of life, and safety. The way you feel while you're awake depends in part on what happens while you're sleeping. During sleep, your body is working to support healthy brain function and maintain your physical health. In children and teens, sleep also helps support growth and development. The damage from sleep deficiency can occur in an instant (such as a car crash), or it can harm you over time. For example, ongoing sleep deficiency can raise your risk for some chronic health problems. It also can affect how well you think, react, work, learn, and get along with others."[36]

Sleep impacts three very important areas of your life. These include:

1. Healthy brain function
2. Emotional well-being
3. Daytime performance and safety

Getting enough sleep is essential to physical well-being. Tom Rath and Jim Harter, PhD, of Gallup compare a good night's sleep to hitting the reset button: "It clears our stressors from the day before. It also increases our chances of having energy and high well-being throughout the day."

If you are constantly tired, you will obviously find yourself behind the eight ball in each of these areas. You become a threat to your own

36 https://zcswellnesscenter.com/ask-the-expert/how-do-poor-habits-effect-my-health/

well-being and the well-being of those around you. It seems so obvious, yet veterans find tremendous challenges in securing the sleep they desperately need. It is not because they don't want to sleep. Who doesn't love sleeping? Rather, it is because they live in a challenging world where their sleep patterns are desperately impacted by powerful brain functions and diseases like PTSD. The trickle-down effect is then much like a snowball rolling downhill. Veterans have trouble navigating their days, completing simple tasks, and maintaining high brain functionality. They start to feel unhappy, anxious, and even depressed. They lose focus, struggle at staying connected with those they love, and start to notice that they are failing at things they once succeeded at. Just like that snowball, it starts small but grows into an uncontrollable force.

Sleep Disturbance[37]

Post-traumatic stress disorder is related to a wide range of medical problems, including neurological, psychological, cardiovascular, respiratory, and gastrointestinal disorders, as well as sleep disorders and diabetes. Although the majority of studies reveal the association between PTSD and sleep disturbances, few studies exist on the assessment of sleep disruption among veterans with PTSD. In this review, they attempted to study the sleep disorders including insomnia, nightmare, sleep-related breathing disorders, sleep-related movement disorders and parasomnias among veterans with chronic war-induced PTSD. It is an important area for further research among veterans with PTSD.

Post-traumatic stress disorder is related to a wide range of medical problems, such as breathing problems, heart disease, mental health, an abnormally active nervous system, and sleep disorders. While an estimated 1–9 percent of the general population has experienced PTSD,

37 https://www.ncbi.nlm.nih.gov/pmc/articles/PMC4967368/#B14

military members are at much greater risk: Between 15–20 percent of enlisted members and veterans will suffer. Sleep disturbance plays a large role here, as difficulty falling and staying asleep and nightmares are all symptoms included in the DSM-IV-TR diagnostic criteria for PTSD. Of those who have PTSD, almost 90 percent complain of sleep disturbance. It could be as insignificant as waking up a few times throughout the night or something much more serious (which is often the case), like the inability to fall asleep, recurrent awakenings, thrashing movements during sleep, or nightmares that cause neurological episodes and distress. A study conducted by the RAND Corporation determined that about 70 percent of deployable service members reported six hours or less of sleep per day; almost half said they slept poorly; one-third felt fatigued three to four times per week.

While treating the underlying cause of PTSD might lead to some improvement in sleep disturbance, most patients are still susceptible to sleep disturbances even after they have found ways to control their PTSD. This shows that sleep deprivation is a regular and secondary symptom of post-traumatic stress disorder—but treating it doesn't necessarily allow veterans to "sleep like a baby." Even as the PTSD might subside, sleep deprivation and dealing with the resulting effects remains very real and completely intact.

Some of the most common sleep disturbances among veterans are:

> **Insomnia.** Insomnia is classified as habitual sleeplessness or the inability to sleep. Insomnia is a common complaint after traumatic events; it causes considerable subjective distress and treatment resistance and is associated with other illnesses among PTSD patients. Veterans with PTSD frequently complain of insomnia.

Nightmares. Nightmares of past or recurring trauma are one of the defining features of PTSD. Nightmares within veterans of PTSD often contain anger, intense terror, grief, guilt, and helplessness. War-zone trauma exposure has shown the strongest correlation with nightmare complaints.

Sleep-related breathing disorders. Sleep-related breathing disorders (SRBD)—repetitive upper airway closure or obstruction during sleep—lead to the stop or decrease of airflow that can force people to wake from sleep to reestablish their breathing. PTSD patients without nightmares breathe more slowly during sleep and exhibit a relative reduction of rate variability during rapid eye movement (REM) sleep, the state from which most nightmares emerge.

Sleep-related movement disorders. These are clinically described as repetitive limb movements that wake the individual. Many times, they occur in response to nightmares or physical issues. Those with PTSD experience movement disorders much more than those without. During one of my sleep studies, they counted more than 270 leg movements in one hour. Whatever else was going on, I'm sure that wasn't restful sleep.

You don't need to be diagnosed with PTSD to suffer from sleep problems and nightmares. Many veterans struggle with sleep when they return. These struggles can quickly escalate to deeper problems, leading to depression and other unexpected conditions. This is where having an expert opinion and medical diagnosis is crucial. Try to self-diagnose yourself with depression that can result from sleep deprivation. You can't. I couldn't tell you when I became depressed, and I certainly couldn't tell you that I was depressed at the time. I can only recognize it in hindsight. The key? Recognize when you're having trouble sleeping and act to improve. This chapter aims to help each veteran understand the importance of sleep, how common the problem is, and how to recognize the seriousness of the condition.

Often, each of these clinical diagnoses and issues are prevalent in veterans suffering from PTSD. In their own way, they each impact and affect sleep patterns and the ability to get a good night's rest. Even one of these recurring ailments could completely change the manner in which you sleep, therefore leaving you feeling restless throughout the day. At its worst, it can cloud your judgment and prevent you from recognizing a traditional form of happiness because you are so tired you cannot see straight. These should not be taken lightly. But clinical issues are not the only threat to good sleep.

Many soldiers with PTSD recognize the following issues as well:[38]

- **They may be "on alert."** Many people with PTSD may feel they need to be on guard or "on the lookout" to protect himself or herself from danger. It is difficult to have restful sleep when you feel the need to be always alert. You might have trouble falling asleep, or you might wake up easily in the night if you hear any noise.
- **They may worry or have negative thoughts.** Your thoughts can make it difficult to fall asleep. People with PTSD often worry about general problems or worry that they are in danger. If you often have trouble getting to sleep, you may start to worry that you won't be able to fall asleep. These thoughts can keep you awake.
- **They may use drugs or alcohol.** Some people with PTSD use drugs or alcohol to help them cope with their symptoms.

38 https://www.clubmentalhealthtalk.com/what-helps-with-ptsd-nightmares/

In fact, using too much alcohol can get in the way of restful sleep. Alcohol changes the quality of your sleep and makes it less refreshing. This is true of many drugs as well.

- **They may have medical problems.** There are medical problems that are commonly found in people with PTSD, such as chronic pain, stomach problems, and pelvic-area problems in women. These physical problems can make going to sleep difficult.

The issues are substantial and real for those regularly threatened with sleep disturbance or deprivation. And like that snowball rolling downhill, the outcomes can be catastrophic. But that doesn't mean there are no solutions or ways in which you can deal with this ongoing and significant problem. In fact, obtaining a good night's sleep might be one of the easiest ways to start living a healthier and more connected life.

The Cure for Sleepless Nights

If anything has improved in my life and improved my happiness, it is my ability to get a good night's sleep. I sought treatment and was surprised to learn that we can work to program nightmares out of our sleep and force our bodies into a routine that starts to drive a good night's rest. For me, the struggle was intense and took several months to improve and more than two years to become almost normal. While writing this chapter, I have experienced a return of some nightmares and some poor sleep. However, instead of feeling fear and frustration, I went back to the healthy sleep habits and routines I developed and learned. I'm much more confident in my ability to cope.

Most importantly, the improvement in my sleep gave me the space I needed to get treatment for the irritability. My wife often laments that she wishes I'd gotten help sooner because the improvement in our marriage and happiness together is immeasurable. Sometimes I falter, but the improvement is unbelievable to me. I went to the VA and committed to doing anything and everything they asked me to do in my treatment. It worked for me.

So, if there is anything you read in this book and take to heart, let it be this chapter and the information that follows. I fear that people will dismiss some things, like not drinking to go to sleep, but it is so important to your overall health and the reward is so great.

The Centers for Disease Control and Prevention estimate that 40.6 million Americans get an inadequate amount of sleep. As you've seen, that number increases amongst veterans. We must work to stop this trend. To start, let's look at some of the traditional steps even the generic bad sleeper can employ to combat some of those sleepless nights. Just like we brush our teeth, shower, and do other things as part of our normal hygiene, we must establish good sleep hygiene. Too much noise, light, or activity in your bedroom can make sleeping harder. Creating a quiet, comfortable sleeping area can help. Consider these commonly recommended actions you can take to sleep better:

- Use your bedroom only for sleeping and sex.
- Move the TV and radio out of your bedroom.
- Keep your bedroom quiet, dark, and cool. Use curtains or blinds to block out light. Consider using soothing music or a "white noise" machine to block out noise. Don't do stressful or energizing things within two hours of going to bed.
- Create a relaxing bedtime routine. You might want to take a warm shower or bath, listen to soothing music, or drink a cup of tea with no caffeine in it.
- Use earplugs and a sleep mask if light and noise bother you.

These are small yet easy steps you can take to reduce some of the smaller threats to your sleep. None of these cures the underlying issues like PTSD, but they work to ensure that you are not compounding the problem. It is also important to have a bedtime routine and schedule. You can program your body to recognize the normal time to go to bed and to wake up. Participating in a sporadic or undefined sleeping schedule can drastically impact your sleeping routine. You really need every advantage you can get.

So, you need to set a time to wake up and keep to it. I was taught that I could hit the snooze button once, but then I had to get up—regardless of how much sleep I received the night before. If I only got three hours of sleep, but I set my alarm for six thirty, then I got up and out of bed. I would do my best to stay awake during the day and try to go to bed at my routine bedtime. My routine started to become more established after about a week of this.

Early on in my treatment and in addition to some of my healthy sleep habits, I was prescribed several sleep medications. While they were crucial to my recovery, I experienced side effects and challenges along the way. My kids would find me sleeping at my computer in another room. On several occasions, my family discovered me sleepwalking. We laugh about those times now, but it wasn't always good. Eventually, I got to the point where I didn't want to use the medication anymore and I weaned myself off of it with the help of my VA docs. I'm better without the meds, and I'm sleeping just fine—95 percent of the time versus 5 percent of the time.

Your daily activities can also impact your sleep patterns. Some tips include:

- **Exercise during the day.** Don't exercise within two hours of going to bed though because it may be harder to fall asleep.
- **Get outside during daylight hours.** Spending time in sunlight helps reset your body's sleep and wake cycles.

- **Cut out or limit what you drink or eat that has caffeine in it**, such as coffee, tea, cola, and chocolate.
- **Don't drink alcohol before bedtime.** Alcohol can make you wake up more often during the night.
- **Don't smoke or use tobacco**, especially in the evening. Nicotine can keep you awake.
- **Don't take naps during the day**, especially close to bedtime.
- **Don't drink any liquids after six p.m. if you wake up often** because you will have to go to the bathroom.
- **Don't take medicine that may keep you awake or make you feel hyper or energized right before bed.** Your doctor can tell you if your medicine may do this and if you can take it earlier in the day.

Your life is a complicated, interconnected puzzle. How you sleep impacts how you thrive and succeed during the day. How you thrive and succeed during the day almost certainly will determine how well you sleep. But on that same note, often PTSD will act like a hurricane and destroy anything and everything in its path, including your ability to sleep well. So, no matter the case, you will almost certainly have to deal with this underlying and tumultuous ailment. The tools in this section should only help supplement the condition of sleep deprivation and your treatment for any underlying PTSD. As you focus on your sleep and work to reestablish a healthy and focused sleeping regimen, you can then shift your attention to your daily activities, which will include an emphasis on wellness.

Wellness: Exercise + Diet + Sleep = Healthy Body

Wellness is an important term for vets. As defined, it means that you are in a state of being in good health, especially as an actively pursued goal. For a host of reasons, many veterans abandon their wellness once they return home from service. At times, they forget about the importance of exercise and a healthy diet as well as the role both of these play in their continued development and health. While in service, most men and women awake each day to rigorous activity and training. They receive carefully assembled food meant to fuel their lives and give them the energy (calories) to operate at a high level. Because of the substantial regimen in serving our country, most of those in the armed forces don't really have to think about when they'll exercise and what they'll eat.

But then they return home and quickly realize that no one is there to feed them or designate the next physical task for them. They are on their own to make decisions for their own health. And that is often when the wheels start to fall off. Wellness is an extremely important facet of the overall mental and physical health of any serviceman or woman attempting to acclimate to civilian life. So, they forego their wellness, which then impacts their minds and bodies at a greater level than they realize.

To that end, our servicemen and women must focus their efforts to include wellness as part of their regimen. That means that they should find time each day to eat right and move around. Writer Sam Collins reports that the US veteran obesity rate has reached 80 percent, surpassing that of the general population. This is a horrifying number. Four out of every five veterans are considered obese, which leads to numerous diseases like diabetes, heart disease, strokes, cancer, and many others. It also impacts confidence, happiness, and your ability to navigate daily responsibilities. More than 20 percent of all veterans suffer from diabetes, which leads to tremendous medical complications and overall health issues.

While the VA is trying to respond by encouraging healthy eating habits and addressing unbalanced dieting, it ultimately falls on the veteran to decide to live a healthy life and focus on wellness. "There are a number of reasons. Food, addictively, works exactly the same neurons in the brain as other addictive substances such as alcohol, and drugs," Michel Goldschmidt, health promotion and disease prevention manager at the Portland VA, told a local NPR member station. "Homelessness, job challenges, PTSD, issues related to their war experiences. That adds up to using what could be considered to be a socially available and acceptable outlet. And eating is one of them.[39]"

Many veterans use food to deal with their emotions and struggles. It is easy, cheap, offers immediate gratification, and is perceived to not be nearly as detrimental to health as substances like alcohol or drugs. Like other post-battle ailments, veterans' weight gain often stems from an uneasy transition to civilian life. While in battle, most veterans need food that is high in fats and carbohydrates to ensure they have enough energy to survive. They burn these off with a high level of physical activity. Goldschmidt and her colleagues also note that soldiers have to eat quickly and generally don't have time to process their hunger level or need for more food. As they return home, they carry these eating habits with them. While their habits served them well on the battlefield, civilian life requires a much healthier alternative.

The CDC says losing as much as 5 percent body weight can reduce the occurrence of obesity-related chronic conditions. Doing so requires at least an hour of daily physical activity and the maintenance of a balanced diet that includes bread, fruit, vegetables, dairy, meat, and fish. The VA is finally recognizing the tremendous need for additional education and implemented a program called MOVE!, a weight management opportunity housed in the federal agency's National Center for Health

39 https://archive.thinkprogress.org/the-veteran-obesity-rate-has-reached-80-percent-what-is-being-done-to-lower-it-fec7e193b0ad/

Promotion and Disease Prevention. But even a positive program like this finds itself limited by a lack of funding and attention. There are just so many other battles to be fought.

The threat is real. In a recent report, A.J. Littman, C.W. Forsberg, and T.D. Koepsell studied the prevalence of physical activity within veterans.[40] Their conclusion: "Despite the high level of physical activity required of active duty military personnel, only a minority of veterans met physical activity recommendations, and the prevalence of inactivity was particularly high in VA users. These findings suggest a large potential to increase activity and improve health in VA users."

The reality is that physical well-being is connected to mental and emotional health. We've said it again and again, but your overall health will always be the culmination of your mind and body. Wellness focuses on diet and exercise, but its benefits directly impact your mind. The healthier your mind, the healthier you will ultimately be. An article on Belongto.com outlines steps to refocus your well-being.[41] These include:

- **Get enough rest.** Having good mental and emotional health requires taking care of your body. That includes getting enough sleep. Most people need seven to eight hours of sleep each night to function optimally.
- **Learn about good nutrition and practice it.** Nutrition is a complicated subject and not always easy to put into practice. You will feel better if you learn about what you eat and how it affects your energy and mood, and if you practice healthy eating habits.
- **Exercise to relieve stress and lift your mood.** Exercise is a powerful antidote to stress, anxiety, and depression. Look for

40 https://www.ncbi.nlm.nih.gov/pubmed/19346987
41 http://www.belongto.org/resource.aspx?contentid=4564

small ways to add activity to your day, like taking the stairs instead of the elevator or going on a short walk. To get the most mental health benefits, aim for thirty minutes or more of exercise per day.

- **Get a dose of sunlight every day.** Sunlight lifts your mood, so try to get at least ten to fifteen minutes of sun per day. You can do this while exercising, gardening, or socializing.
- **Limit alcohol and avoid cigarettes and other drugs.** These unhealthy outlets are addictive and can damage your body and overall health.

This is just a starting point. Thriving is not just the absence of disease or illness. Rather, it is finding and maintaining the ability to enjoy life with ease. Veterans often think of traditional mechanisms for physical activity, like going to the gym, lifting weights, and running. But the options are endless: walking the dog, jogging with a loved one, playing outside with your kids, going to the mall, enjoying the park, swimming, kayaking, cycling, playing team sports like basketball or baseball or individual sports like tennis or golf, and much more. The point: Movement equals wellness.

More and more employers are realizing the great opportunity in ensuring their employees engage in a healthy, happy lifestyle. They are promoting healthy living options, diet, and, of course, movement. These same principles and attitudes should be applied to veterans after completing their service.

Tom Rath and Jim Harter, PhD, report that just 38 percent of people in their studies exercised or had a lot of physical activity in the past day. Among 400,000 Americans surveyed, only 27 percent got the recommended thirty minutes or more of exercise five days per week. They also found that people who exercise at least two days per week are happier and experience less stress than those who don't. Each additional day of exercise boosts energy levels. So, while it may seem counterintuitive at first glance, exercise is one of the best ways to combat fatigue.

Rath and Harter also report that a recent experiment of theirs revealed that just twenty minutes of exercise could improve mood for several hours *after* working out. Researchers monitored participants who rode a bike at moderate intensity and another group that did not exercise. Those who exercised for just twenty minutes had a significant improvement in their mood after two, four, eight, and twelve hours when compared to those who did not exercise.[42] In fact, a comprehensive analysis of more than seventy trials found that *exercising is much more effective at eliminating fatigue than prescription drugs* used for this purpose. Think about that for a second. Most veterans turn to prescription meds and self-medication like alcohol and drugs, when working out is the best (and safest) cure for their fatigue and sleepless nights.

As veterans return to home and work to fold back into a normal civilian lifestyle, many report that they have trouble finding their place in society. They lack purpose and goals and then lose self-esteem and confidence. This impacts their overall wellness. Researchers at Columbia University found that psychological perceptions of one's body image could be as important as objective measures like body mass index (BMI). That translates into the notion that healthy bodies lead to a positive outlook on life and greater self-confidence.

In their book *Wellbeing: The Five Essential Elements*, Rath and Harter outline the findings of Gallup scientists, who have studied the demands of living a full life. While this has been an ongoing study spanning more than fifty years, more recently, in partnership with leading

42 http://www.gallup.com/businessjournal/127211/exercise-sleep-physical-wellbeing.aspx

economists, psychologists, and other acclaimed scientists, Gallup has uncovered the common elements of well-being that transcend countries and cultures. This research revealed the universal elements of well-being that differentiate a thriving life from one spent suffering. They represent five broad categories that are essential to most people:[43]

- **Career Well-being:** how you occupy your time—or simply liking what you do every day
- **Social Well-being:** having strong relationships and love in your life
- **Financial Well-being:** effectively managing your economic life
- **Physical Well-being:** having good health and enough energy to get things done on a daily basis
- **Community Well-being:** the sense of engagement you have with the area where you live

Each of these five areas of well-being is an essential part of any full, meaningful life. We could probably write a book about each one. But the crucial takeaway is to be aware of how each of these areas can play an important role in your overall happiness and development. If you lack even one area, you'll likely find yourself feeling a degree of regret or need for improvement. For this chapter, we have predominantly focused on your physical well-being, which has encompassed an initial focus on creating healthy sleep patterns at night and healthy eating and exercise patterns during the day.

They are interconnected and do not exist in a vacuum. You'll find little reprieve in your daily activities without a good night's sleep. And maximizing your daily movement and eating habits will simultaneously

43 http://www.gallup.com/businessjournal/126884/five-essential-elements-wellbeing.aspx

help you get a good night's rest. Most veterans return home from their service programmed to operate in a very specific manner that supports their needs as servicemen and women. They aren't afforded many good nights of sleep, often have to eat their meals rather quickly with little socialization, and use food as fuel, rather than for wellness. They then return home to a different life, one without the structure and regimen of their time in service. But they simply cannot flip the switch and turn off all that they once knew. So, they find trouble in introducing exercise, wellness, and sleep into their daily routines.

Many underlying concerns and ailments impact sleep and overall well-being. So, veterans should work to achieve balance in their lives and constantly work to recapture their wellness.

Chapter 6

RECONNECTING WITH SUPPORT AT HOME:

Friends and Family Matter

As you reconnect with your own physical well-being, work on connecting with your support system that surrounds you too. Each and every veteran has his or her homecoming story. Nothing makes for better media than a returning vet on TV with his or her loved one in their arms—the embrace that has waited for months, the impassioned kiss that is almost like their first love's kiss. It's almost like a black-and-white '40s movie and the most romantic scene on the screen. Whether it's a veteran cleverly masked as a baseball catcher reuniting with his son at the pitcher's mound or the pregnant wife running across the tarmac to be swooped up by the handsome soldier in his desert camo battle dress uniform (BDU). The warm embrace and the warmed hearts at home with misty eyes and the feeling, like—ah, true love and happily ever after.

When I returned from Diego Garcia in 1991, I could see her from a mile away as I walked down the airstairs. I couldn't wait to get to her. My heart was beating out of my chest. I'd been cooped up in a C-141 from Germany in the midst of all kinds of excitement from everyone on the plane. Everybody wanted to be home. So, when I saw her, I couldn't think of anything else but to get to her. And, as soon as we connected, boom, a camera appeared about three inches from my face. The man holding it started to walk around us so he could get all the footage to make the six o'clock news. I just wanted to be with her, so the camera was so out of place and such a distraction. Already, two stories were underway. One for the news channel and one for our real lives.

The story the media and America wanted was the sweet sight of the reunion—short, impactful images and a few sound bites. The story between my wife and me was completely different. It was about us, it was about adjustment; it was going to last much longer than the twenty-second video clip could portray. Our story was about reconnecting and everything that went with my transition back into regular life and our transition back together. That is a similar story for almost every returning troop. But very few of these stories play out on television in the same way. Many veterans find themselves stuck in despair and the fresh wounds of their recent deployment. They suffer from PTSD. It isn't easy to adjust or reconnect with the most important people in their lives—family and friends.

Veterans are not alone in their deployment. Their spouses, family, friends, and even their dogs share in the physical and emotional pain of being away from one another. Frequently they've undergone extreme experiences, which they often cannot cope with alone. They are changed, and so are the ones who stayed behind awaiting their return. So, we can only help veterans reconnect through an entire family approach. Many veterans mistakenly and unintentionally go about it with the "go at it alone" mentality. They say, "I can fix this." But in truth, they cannot do it alone. They need help, and this chapter will assist all of us in that crucial process. In his article, "Helping Veterans Reconnect with Home," Montgomery C. Meigs writes[44]:

At a recent dinner in New York's Gotham Hall, Adm. Mike Mullen, the chairman of the Joint Chiefs of Staff, poignantly described a lot of veterans of our campaigns in Southwest Asia. Returning home, Mullen said, they encounter a society from which their service has in a way estranged them. Can we help them if we do not understand what they and their families need as they make their transition back to civilian life?

Our servicemen and women and their families accept as routine psychological and physical trauma that most Americans never see. Mullen spoke of Annette Kuyper, the mother of a National Guardsman, who said, 'We closed the blinds on the windows overlooking the driveway so we don't see the Army vehicle arriving with a chaplain bearing the unbearable news.' Imagine the night before deploying to a combat zone, telling a son or daughter, a high-schooler approaching adulthood perhaps, that if a military vehicle drives up and a chaplain and an officer of higher rank get out, it is time to stand by their remaining parent. Try to put yourself in the shoes of a single parent who must not only leave his or her children with parents or friends for 15 months but who must also live with the reality that the children may not see him or her again. Unlike military families, the average American does not live with this dread of the knock on the door.

---

44 https://www.washingtonpost.com/wpdyn/content/article/2010/11/12/AR2010111206452.html

Those who serve in harm's way sustain these psychological scars, often with no complaint. As Mullen put it, 'They're a very proud group. They don't always show that they are struggling, and they are guarded when it comes to talking about their needs. One Iraq veteran says, 'You don't ask for help. You think you can do it and you think you can handle it, because that's what you're trained to do.'

... But as we've all seen, that is not always the case. I recently listened to an interview with a former soldier named Reagan[45] (his full name is not provided), who shared that he was not the same after returning home from Iraq. In his own words:

Reagan: When I got home, I was doing pretty good. I thought I hit the ground running. My third day home, I had already had a full-time job locked on and I started working every day. I worked actually three months before I even took a day off. I stayed really busy and everything seemed to be going pretty good, until I started to have some downtime. I actually got promoted at my job, didn't have to work seven days a week. I think that's when I started noticing a little difference in basically who I was. I was a lot more irritable. I was always tired. I never slept. I actually got pulled over one time for failure to maintain a lane. It was actually kind of embarrassing to me at the time, because the police thought I was drunk, or inebriated, or talking on the cellphone.

I said, "No." What had happened was there was a bag in the road and I just didn't even think about it. I just assumed it was an IED. I mean, subconsciously I swerved to miss it. There was a police officer right

45 https://www.maketheconnection.net/contentassets/fd0ebf8c414946648292552f2c3a0721/im-not-the-same-person-i-was-before-iraq.pdf

behind me, he flipped the lights, and he wanted to know what's going on. I didn't even tell him that. I just told him, "I don't know. I didn't maintain my lane." I didn't want him to think I was crazy. I didn't want him to think, *Wow, what's the deal with this guy?*

Then I just noticed that my relationship with everybody as time went on, it got worse. I was harder to deal with. It got to the point where I was almost impossible to deal with. I was having trouble at work. I ended up losing the job because I was getting violent. I was really irritable, hard to deal with. Then a friend of mine that I worked with, his dad came into town, and we were talking about the military and my service. He was in the Navy back in the day and we were talking about that and everything. He was kind of telling me, "Do you have any problems?" I said, "It's funny. I kind of do." He was the one that told me, "You need to get with the VA. You need to go see somebody. You need to get help." I was like, "Nah, I don't need that.' He's like, 'You do, you really do. I'm telling you now, you do.' " It's like he knew something that I didn't, because he had already been there. Since I've really started getting help, my life isn't perfect by no means.

There's no doubt in my mind, I'm not the same person that I was before I went to Iraq. It's just, I'm not that person anymore. But I eventually came to the conclusion that I can either throw in the towel and fall to the wayside, or I can get every bit of help that I can and become the best person I can be right now. I'm engaged now. I want the best life for me and her. We have two kids. I want the best life for them. If it's a struggle with me every day, then it's going to be a struggle. All I can do is to get the help I need.

We got into an argument one time and I said, "It might really help you understand me and some of the ways I am if you understood PTSD ... It just might help you understand. You might be a little more sympathetic at times, but you're going to need to know what's possibly going on with me." I wanted her and myself, "Let's get in front of somebody because maybe I am making excuses for myself. Maybe I'm not, but let's get someone else's opinion other than mine."

She did some research on it and then she started to get an idea of what it was. Then we went to the vet center in Spring, Texas, and we started talking to somebody out there as a couple. Her being supportive has made a huge difference. Everything's not perfect. We still have our struggles, but it's a lot better when you're educated on what's going on.

For three years when I got home, I didn't want to talk to nobody. I just stayed busy. I blanked it out. But guess what? It doesn't go anywhere. It's there. You're going to run, but you're going to get tired sooner or later and that problem is gonna be there. If you have an opportunity to go talk to somebody, you need to go do it. Anytime you want, pick up a phone, go to a center, anything. Go talk to somebody. Because whatever you're dealing with, you think you're the only one. You think I'm on this island all alone. There's a thousand more people going through the same thing, and it will benefit you. It will benefit them to talk about it. "Hey, this works for me. What works for you?" Mix and mingle and figure out what's best. And just realize, you know what, the situation I'm going through, it really isn't cool, but I'm not the only one. I'm not alone. This is really normal, and let's get some help. Let's do this.

All in the Family

The struggles each of these families experience when a loved one is dealing with PTSD are very present and extremely powerful. Telltale signs of deep-seated emotional impact stem directly from the challenges of serving our country. Some of these emotions come from family members;

others come from the veteran themselves. In fact, many families dealing with these issues can experience one if not more of the following:[46]

Sympathy. You may feel sorry for your loved one's suffering. This may help your loved one know that you sympathize with him or her. However, be careful that you are not treating him or her like a permanently disabled person. With help, they can feel better.

Negative Feelings. PTSD can make someone seem like a different person. If you believe your family member no longer has the traits you loved, it may be hard to feel good about them. Avoid negative feelings by educating yourself about PTSD. Even if your loved one refuses treatment, you will probably benefit from some support.

Avoidance. Avoidance is a symptom of PTSD. People with PTSD avoid situations and reminders of their trauma. As a family member, you may be avoiding the same things as your loved one. Or, you may be afraid of their reaction to certain cues. One possible solution is to do some social activities, but let your family member stay home if they wish. However, they might be so afraid for your safety that you also can't go out. If so, seek professional help.

Depression. This is common among family members when the person with PTSD causes feelings of pain or loss. When PTSD lasts for a long time, you may begin to lose hope that your family will ever "get back to normal."

Anger and Guilt. If you feel responsible for your family member's happiness, you may feel guilty when you can't make a difference. You could also be angry if they can't keep a job or drink too much or because they are angry or irritable. You and your loved one must get past this anger and guilt by understanding that the feelings are no one's fault.

---

46 https://www.nsfamilyline.org/ptsd

Health problems. Everyone's bad habits, such as drinking, smoking, and not exercising, can get worse when trying to cope with their family member's PTSD symptoms. You may also develop other health problems when you're constantly worried, angry, or depressed.

Even one of these unintended consequences of service could have a tremendous impact on your life and family dynamic. It can change how you relate, communicate, interact, and exist together. If you find your loved one experiencing even one of these issues, it is extremely important to respond to them and address them as soon as you can.

Resilience: Coping with Reconnection

As our brave troops return home, they often have to confront the demons of their service. PTSD can be lurking in the shadows, acting as a difficult obstacle to their journey toward finding love and connection with family and friends. PTSD may include nightmares, flashbacks, hyperarousal, anger, and depression, just to name a few of the many potential emotions. To stop the symptoms, you must treat the ailment. "PTSD tends to wreak havoc on intimate relationships," says psychologist Candice Monson, PhD, deputy director of the women's health sciences division of the National Center for Posttraumatic Stress Disorder.

Marine Brian Escobedo shared his experience with me:

My name is Brian Escobedo. I was born and raised here in Houston, Texas. I spent five years in the Marine Corps and got out as a sergeant with three tours in Iraq. Everybody knew me as just the happiest dude. Even in the Marine Corps, I was always the funny dude, making everybody laugh; but there was a time where there was just no laughing. On my second deployment, I got hit three times. Four bombs hit my vehicle. For me to survive in that environment, under those extreme emotional conditions where I was just living in fear, living with anxiety, I had to go emotionally numb.

I didn't realize how messed up I was until I got back to America. I started having pretty horrible nightmares, and I couldn't focus on anything. I was having constant flashbacks. The whole time I was awake, I was miserable. I was angry. I couldn't feel any excitement about life. Nothing. I stopped listening to music. I stopped talking so much to my friends. I isolated myself. I would just stay in my room all day and just drink and drink and drink and drink, and I didn't know why. I knew I had PTSD, but I didn't know that I'd be scared to drive, just drive on a simple American road. You become suspicious of everything, like mounds of trash, dead animals, everything ... You're expecting everything to be booby-trapped, and when you start thinking like that, everything seems like a threat in your environment. It kind of makes you go nuts.

As military people, you find it very difficult to admit your own weaknesses because that's also completely contrary to military philosophy. So when you have PTSD or you have anything like that or any sort of emotional stress, you just suck it up. I actually moved in with my brother when I got back from the Marine Corps, and he understood me very well. He was very patient with me. I was isolating myself and all the typical things that people with PTSD do, and he helped me out. I've been to one-on-one psychologists at the VA. I've been to multiple different forms of therapy. You have to surround yourself with good people that want to see you do better, and you have to take advantage of the programs at the VA or the nonprofit organizations that are there to help veterans out.

I forgot that there was good in the world, and every time I saw Rebecca, it brought it back. It was like, *Oh, this is the reason I'm going to live. This is the reason that I shouldn't do anything crazy to myself.* It just starts with saying, "You know what? I want to fix this." Takes a lot of courage to go against that military training that you have to admit that there's something that's broken inside you and you need to fix it. That's the very first step. It all starts with going to the VA, and there's a whole community of veterans that just want to help you out, people that have been in your same shoes, that know what you're going through, that have already overcome this. You just reach your hand out and connect to somebody else that knows what you're going through and knows how to help you. You know, that's all it takes.

Brian's story is a tremendous example of how a man troubled by his past was unwilling to let it impact his future. He is loved, cared for, and surrounded by family who wants to help him recover and reconnect. Most veterans return home to a strong support system. But loved ones not only need to understand how to help but also to recognize it will take patience and considerable effort to do so. Elizabeth Carll, PhD, has developed and outlined some valuable approaches to working with families that have a member suffering from PTSD. In her two-volume work, *Trauma Psychology: Issues in Violence, Disaster, Health, and Illness,* she shares some of the most effective strategies to combat PTSD and help family members reconnect.

These include:

- **Teaching stress-management skills.** Everyone responds to stress in a different manner. Family members and the vet need to recognize how the veteran is dealing with the present situation. Some turn to alcohol or other unhealthy practices, while others find healthy mechanisms like working out, enjoying time with their children, or finding a new profession or hobby.

- **Using families' previously effective coping skills to build a framework for present and future resilience.** Likely at some point, you and your family worked through problems in a healthy manner. It is time to figure out how you did so and acclimatize your family members to that.
- **Discussing how the traumatized person and family members want to address the event with people outside the family.** This concept is particularly important in the case of emotionally loaded traumas. Sometimes people need time. In other situations, a vet may be immediately ready to spend more time with people outside of the household. Consider these conversations before you push the envelope further than you should.
- **Helping the family to understand that the event has impacted *everyone*, even if that is not apparent at first.** Most families feel as if they must focus on the needs of only the returning troop, and that is quite important. But service is a family sacrifice. You have to recognize (as a family) that everyone has specific needs and pain points as a soldier returns home.
- **Treatment is not just limited to the soldier.** The entire family, in varying degrees, should be folded into the treatment program. Otherwise, someone might feel left out or get left behind.
- **Understanding that men and women, as well as individuals, process trauma differently.** Women may want to talk about it more, for example, while men may shut down or take their feelings out through exercise or activity. The bigger point here might be that we all deal with trauma in a unique way. Families should use the fundamental principles just outlined while remaining flexible as needed.

Tiffany, the fiancée of a recent serviceman, shared with me the following when referring to her future husband, Reagan:

TIFFANY: He wants, just like any man wants, the very best for his family. It took a lot because he thought he was strong enough to handle it; but he realizes that actually, the wise, manly thing to do is to go get some help because we all need help sometimes and it doesn't make us any less of a Marine, in his case, or any less of a man or any less of a human. Humanness is supporting one another and working through those really traumatic situations so that you can power through and move forward with a much more pleasant, healthy, whatever-normal-is-for-you and your-family kind of life. I would say to fellow spouses or loved ones of a veteran that it takes gentle prodding. It takes a gentle, constant push because a veteran doesn't always ask because they're used to being the one that's turned to in the time of need. That's their call of duty.

I think our call of duty is as the support system is to not allow it to go unseen and continue to help them find the value that isn't always seen. It's about really understanding that person that's going through some of those symptoms, some of the areas that we can't all understand and just helping boost them and giving them the tools that they need in order to manage it themselves.

While the VA hospital is a remarkable tool for the soldier, it does not currently offer family treatment, which focuses on the dynamic and interaction of the entire household. If we are going to be the difference in the development and reacclimatization of our beloved troops, we have to focus on a collaborative effort to work through the changes and challenges as a family/friend unit.

Resilience is the ability to withstand and rebound from disruptive life challenges. Service, deployment, and war are extremely disruptive and change any and all who volunteer for these tremendous responsibilities. But for just as many problems that may occur for a troop trying to reconnect, there are just as many ways that a strong family dynamic and support system can reduce the strain and help soldiers recover. Patience, perseverance, and human resilience often act as the antidotes to these difficult times.

Chapter 7

FINDING A NEW MISSION AND NEW PURPOSE:

An Identity After Service

As you reconnect with your new version of life, your continued development and growth will flourish if you find a new mission and purpose. As servicemen and women, your lives are filled with responsibility and purpose, a situation at least partially created by the military system. You must adhere to boundaries, rules, guidelines, and (frankly) a jam-packed schedule. You signed up for a very singular goal, and anything and everything you do is designed to help you achieve that outlined target.

When you enlist, you agree to join the largest team on Earth, and often your mission is based on the needs of your country. It can change on a daily basis, or your role can remain the same for your entire length of service. But if nothing else, there is no lacking in purpose. Realistically, you have applied for and been hired for one of the most important jobs in the world—to protect our country. Talk about a significant job description. Every single thing you do moves you closer and closer to your mission and your purpose. From your training to every interaction, it is all carefully curated to serve the role you play in protecting the US.

No doubt you enlisted because you believe in and want to protect the fundamental pillars that built America. If you are brave and courageous enough to risk your life to serve others, we can only assume that you are not just mission-driven but believe deep down in your heart that your purpose is to protect and serve. Waking up with that level of dedication is extraordinarily inspiring and likely one of the purest forms of expression on Earth. Life has meaning, but there is little in life that has meaning like this. Just ask yourself what else you'd give your life for. You probably have a small list that may not include anything other than your family.

But the beauty of mission- and purpose-driven service may also be one of the greatest challenges for any serviceman or woman. As much purpose as they have while serving, it is extremely difficult to replace this once their service ends and they transition back to civilian life. Consequently, many veterans find themselves feeling empty inside, constantly looking for that same fulfilling feeling but falling short wherever they look. No nine-to-five desk or office job can offer the same rush and emotion that fighting for your country or fighting alongside your buddies gives you. You've felt the deep-seated connection, and very little might serve in its place.

So, the result? Plenty of passionate servicemen and women wonder how they'll ever find a new, meaningful mission. In truth, you may not ever reach that same level of connectivity with your jobs or responsibilities—but that doesn't mean you shouldn't try to fill the gap. This chapter will help you better understand the importance of mission and purpose while you work to figure out how you can adjust to your new life and transition into a civilian version of the same.

Understanding Mission and Purpose

One of the most effective ways to begin finding a new mission and purpose is to first understand the definition and difference of each. From a navigator's perspective, a personal mission is a compass for your day-to-day life. It helps you make decisions to stay on track. This is somewhat different than the missions you had in the military. Your new personal mission is as well defined, but you probably carry it out over a longer time. As you transition back to civilian life, you have to first understand that you are no longer on a military type of mission; but that shouldn't limit you from working toward your goals.

We would rarely refer to creating a proposal, budgeting, or building a new website as a mission. That's a job. And that's okay. Jobs and missions do share something—each requires that you work with others to reach a certain goal. The real difference is what's really at stake if you fail. Approaching a job like a mission can help you remain connected, dedicated, and task oriented, but probably your job will never fulfill you the way your mission might have. Understanding that will help you set appropriate expectations and avoid the letdown that can naturally occur.

I would suggest the following mission to begin your transition. **Your new mission is:**

To overcome whatever adversity you face and find a new purpose or passion and pursue it with every fiber of your being. Nothing will stop you from success. You will work with others and do the necessary things to find happiness. You will not try to go it alone.

Purpose is a little different than mission. Purpose is the reason for which something is done or created or for which something exists: a person's sense of resolve or determination. You don't always create your mission, but you do manifest your purpose. You get to choose what offers you resolve; it is your call to find your motivation or inspiration for it. You likely joined the Army, Navy, Marines, or Air Force because you felt a sense of purpose that aligned with their mission. So, mission is external and often given to you, while purpose is internal and often created by you. That is an important distinction because you can easily create purpose once you return home from your service. All it takes is connecting to something that carries personal meaning to you.

It doesn't have to be some spectacular high-stakes job. It could be almost anything that motivates you and keeps you headed in the right direction. For example, I know someone who volunteered at a local Humane Society once he returned home from his service. He was a K-9 officer in the Army and loved to be around animals. While his mission might have shifted, he found purpose in helping dogs and cats find worthy homes. The point? So many ways exist to find your purpose, and no opportunity is too small. Regardless what you choose, make a choice. Maintaining mission and purpose will help you live a meaningful, fulfilling life.

My purpose has been to save people's lives or help people heal through the medical devices my company designs or manufactures and sell to the healthcare industry. Not only that, I've found my purpose in finding ways to change the lives of the people who work with me by helping them create wealth and success as they define it. I get more personal reward from seeing other people becoming successful than anything I experience toward my own benefit.

The Benefit of Purpose

In his article "The Power of Purpose," Spencer Kympton says:[47]

Purpose compels us to act. Purpose drives us to achieve. Purpose shapes our identity, and this identity then impacts how we pursue our professions, our communities, our education, and our ideals. At the center of the human spirit lies purpose. After their military service, many veterans struggle to find purpose without the structure, mission, and camaraderie of a military unit. It is time we help them find it again.

For the 5 million Americans who have voluntarily served in uniform since 9/11, their time spent serving in the military has been richly defined by purpose. For countless enlistees, cadets, and officer candidates, military service begins with a demonstrated commitment to serving our country. It is codified in their oath of enlistment. It is tested during their training. It is shared with others when they join their units and execute their missions. And for more than 2 million of them over the last decade, their commitment to serve has taken them to Iraq, Afghanistan, or the surrounding Middle East where their purpose has been forged alongside their comrades-in-arms in the deserts and mountains and streets and seas of the Middle East.

Strip a person of purpose, and you leave them with a void—emotional, spiritual, and/or physical. The first-time marathon runner may be unprepared for the void they experience after they cross the finish line. The recent retiree may languish on the backside of the milestone they sought for years. The runner and the retiree alike are experiencing life without the purpose that once drove them.

Spencer brings the heart of the matter to light. Examples abound everywhere. Spencer outlined a few in his article:

47 https://www.huffpost.com/entry/post_2622_b_1076997

- Adam Burke uses his farming as a means to help fellow veterans recover from their injuries.
- Amanda Heidenreiter found purpose again by training service dogs for disabled veterans.
- Anthony Smith tackled his extreme physical and emotional wounds by teaching martial arts to at-risk youth.

Each of these examples shows how servicemen and women have found a way to connect with inspiring and motivating opportunities at home. A great article by Shelley Prevost published on Inc.com, entitled "5 Reasons Why People Never Discover Their Purpose,"[48] indicates those five reasons:

1. **You live from the outside in, not the inside out.** "People are taught from a very young age to look to others for guidance. Social norming is an important part of childhood—you figure out how to act in relation to everyone else—but the problem begins when you extend that process to include something as personal as your life purpose."
2. **You look for a career before you listen for a calling.** "Finding your purpose is about listening to an inner calling. In 'Let Your Life Speak,' Parker Palmer says that we should let our life speak to us, not tell our life what we're going to do with it."
3. **You hate silence.** "Silence muffles the noise and creates a space for authenticity to surface. In silence, you can ask yourself questions about how your life and work are *really* going

48 https://www.inc.com/shelley-prevost/5-reasons-why-most-people-never-discover-their-purpose.html

and pause to wait for the answer. In silence, you give the data of your life the time to converge into a few lessons."

4. **You don't like the dark side of yourself.** "It's the underbelly of your personality that you'd rather others not see. It represents your deficiencies, your failures, and your selfish drives. Most of us flee before anyone has the chance to see this side. But here's the thing: the part of you that's darkest has the most to teach you about your purpose. If discovering your purpose is really about self-discovery, your darkness shows you where you most need to grow."
5. **You devalue the unconscious mind.** "To discover your purpose, you must get comfortable with the non-logical mind. You must become accustomed to not having the answers. You must tolerate ambiguity and get OK with struggling. You must allow yourself to feel—deeply feel. *Thinking* your way to a purposeful life will never work."

If any of these reasons resonate with you and your actions or inactions, you are likely suffering from your limiting beliefs. We are all ingrained and created to desire purpose. But sometimes life—or our mindsets—can prevent us from fully recognizing purpose. And that is just for the common guy or gal that hasn't been impacted by enlisting and serving our country. Sprinkle that on top, and it can get even more complicated. Purpose is seriously powerful stuff.

Patrick Hill, an assistant professor of psychology at Carleton University in Ottawa, Canada, looked at data from the Midlife in the United States (MIDUS) study, funded by the National Institute on Aging.[49] He

49 https://www.npr.org/sections/health-shots/2014/07/28/334447274/people-who-feel-they-have-a-purpose-in-life-live-longer

and his colleague Nicholas Turiano looked at 6,000 people and asked them to answer questions that gauged positive and negative emotions. They found that fourteen years after those questions were asked, people who had reported a greater sense of purpose and direction were more likely to outlive their peers. The study showed that people with a sense of purpose had a 15 percent lower risk of death compared to those that didn't feel as if they found purpose. The best part? It didn't matter at what point in their lives they found purpose—just that they found it. Hill's analysis controlled for other factors known to affect longevity, things like age, gender, and emotional well-being. A sense of purpose trumped all that. Hill defines it as providing something like a "compass or lighthouse that provides an overarching aim and direction in day-to-day lives."

The numbers don't lie. Purpose not only keeps you connected, it keeps you alive. Friedrich Nietzsche said, "He who has a why to live for can bear almost any how." You can find purpose, even after you leave your service and transition into civilian life. The question is not if you can, the question is whether you will.

Buzz Aldrin and His Struggles to Find New Purpose[50]

In the months that followed his return to Earth from his historic voyage on *Apollo 11*, Buzz Aldrin struggled to answer the question asked everywhere he went: "What was it like to be on the moon?" How can someone explain something like that? How can you find a higher mountain to climb?

His reentry into life after the moon was a roller coaster of wins and defeats. At first, Aldrin experienced ticker-tape parades and meetings with heads of state. He received the Medal of Freedom and recogni-

50 https://www.biography.com/news/buzz-aldrin-alcoholism-depression-moon-landing

tion for his great NASA accomplishments, which were many. He had experienced what only one other person on Earth had experienced until then—and only a few since.

He had successes; however, these activities did not fulfill him. And after nearly twenty years in the Air Force and another seven with NASA, the career serviceman was heading into an abyss. He wrote in *Magnificent Desolation*, "There was no goal, no sense of calling, no project worth pouring myself into." Miserable, Aldrin began drinking more, some days not bothering to get out of bed, and put his marriage on shaky ground by seeking solace in the arms of another woman.

The dreaded feelings of hopelessness and despair had overwhelmed him. He confided in the base flight surgeon, who referred him to another doctor at Brooke Army Medical Center in San Antonio, Texas. Finally, Aldrin had the opportunity to open up about the aimlessness that had engulfed him for nearly two years and to delve into deeper-rooted problems, including the pressures of pleasing his father and a family history of mental illness that included the suicides of his mother and grandfather.

Shortly before he formally retired from the Air Force on March 1, 1972, Aldrin publicly revealed his difficulties in an *LA Times* article titled, "Troubled Odyssey—'Buzz' Aldrin's Saga: Tough Role for Hero." Afterward, letters of encouragement he received heartened him and he agreed to serve on the board of directors of the National Association for Mental Health (NAMH). He toured the country to speak of his personal experiences with depression. However, his drinking had also spiraled out of control, rendering him an unreliable option to show up for scheduled engagements.

Aldrin then checked into an alcohol rehabilitation center in August 1975. It wasn't enough. By the end of 1976, he was headed for his second divorce. He reentered Alcoholics Anonymous just before rock bottom came. Aldrin, in a drunken rage, was arrested for smashing in the door of his girlfriend's apartment. Disgusted with himself for being back at square one, he gave up the bottle for good in October 1978.

More difficulties and heartbreak would come, but from that point, Aldrin was able to rediscover purpose in his life: as an aide to recovering alcoholics, an author, a continued contributor to the American space program, and, finally, as a symbol of the great era of space exploration that had once placed on him a burden almost too great to bear.

Searching for Purpose

Imagine just returning from a lengthy deployment. Over the course of the past few years, maybe even more, you have found yourself living an extraordinarily regimented life. In some fashion, the government and military planned nearly every waking moment of your existence. From the moment you started your day till the moment you hit your pillow late in the evening, your mission, whatever it might be, was outlined and expected to be executed. Mission was easy. It was offered to you on a silver platter.

But purpose is something else. Likely, you enlisted because you found great connection and meaning in your desire to serve this country. It was a purposeful endeavor for you. As you spent time overseas or in the United States handling domestic affairs, you likely found your purpose to transform and morph into something else. At the heart of the matter and ingrained into your fabric was your deep-seated desire to protect and to serve. However, as you dove even deeper, you likely found yourself facing an even greater purpose—or at least one more readily defined.

For example, many frontliners have told me that they joined the Army to go overseas and protect our country from imminent terroristic threats. But as they spent time in a foreign country and saw its beauty and true need for assistance, they shifted their purpose not just to protecting things at home but to caring for the local men, women, and children who desperately needed protection and the bare necessities for survival too. Purpose changed, albeit inadvertently, but it was purpose nonetheless.

I cannot understate the importance of purpose. As you return home, you might not find the same purpose you had prior to your enlistment. But that feeling of purpose is still something for which you likely strive. It fills you up, and you might be left looking to find something to replace all the purpose and connection you very recently felt. Buddha said, "Your purpose in life is to find your purpose and give your whole heart and soul to it." To that end, consider some of the most effective ways to find your purpose once you return home:

1. **Start with connection and passion.** The most purposeful things in your life are those with which you feel a genuine connection. You think about them often, and likely they keep you up at night. What are you passionate about? What do you absolutely love to do? What doesn't feel like work to do? If the answer is at the tip of your tongue, you are likely getting closer and closer to your purpose. Don't be discouraged if the answer isn't right there.
2. **Find purposeful work.** On many occasions, I hear about veterans returning home and accepting remedial jobs that don't excite them. They do them because they help pass time, give them something to wake up for, and pay the bills. That's not purpose. That's just work. Your work should align with your purpose, especially when you are doing it for at least eight hours a day and forty hours each week. I am not saying that every job you

have will be purposeful, but I am saying that you should look for jobs that mean something to you. Regardless, pursue your work with passion because it creates the habits you'll need when you find your true passion in life.

3. **Supplement your work with purposeful endeavors.** Even if you are working a job that might not feel all that purposeful, that doesn't mean you should simply settle for a life without connection. Each day has twenty-four hours, and you aren't spending every last one of them at your job. What does that mean for you? Partake in opportunities to volunteer, connect with local vets, serve in church groups, and shift from serving your country to serving your community.
4. **Surround yourself with friends and family.** More so than just about anything else, your loved ones will inspire purpose and help you remain connected internally and externally. If you have younger children, just think of the joy they will bring you as you invest more time in their lives. They need you, and you need them. Your significant other, if you have one, is also a wonderful purpose generator. The shared love and time together can be truly inspiring.
5. **Be mindful.** Mindfulness is all the craze these days, but it really does have tremendous benefits. Yoga, meditation, quiet time, therapy, working out, reading, or going for a long and peaceful walk can all generate a great deal of purpose. It will allow you to reflect, ponder, wonder, think, and gain valuable insight into your feelings and emotions. Purpose is everywhere, and you never know what mindful experience will lead you to it.
6. **Look to your past.** Sometimes, past performance does predict future results. If you are having trouble finding your connection

and purpose upon returning home from service, look at your past to consider those engaging opportunities that offered you purpose in the first place. If you were in computer technology in the military, you might really enjoy coding or website development. If you faced combat in the Army, doing physical activity might be the best option for you. Consider activities that offered you a sense of purpose in the past to act as a guiding light to re-engage you to your future purpose.

7. **Don't give up.** It can take time to fill the void your service left inside of you. In fact, you might feel as if nothing will ever fill that void. Likely, that is at least partly why many servicemen and women accept additional deployments. They want to find that rush of purpose again. It is quite common to take time to find your true calling and really feel that sense of connection upon returning home. Don't rush it. Understand that it is a process. Honor that, and don't give up before you find your purpose.

But don't stop there …

Shannon Kaiser authored the article "3 Unexpected Ways to Find Purpose in Life." She outlines a few additional and surprising ways to find connection:[51]

1. **Get More Action.** You can't think your way into finding your life purpose; you have to do your way into it. Take a mental note from Nike and Just Do It. The more we act, the more we get clear on things. So instead of overthinking it—Will this work out? Should I try that? What if I don't like it? What if I don't

51 https://www.huffingtonpost.com/shannon-kaiser/3-unexpected-ways-to-find_b_5176511.html

make money at it? Start taking steps toward your goals and start trying new things. This will help you get out of your own way. I struggled for years trying to find out what my purpose was. This cycle only created a deeper lack of clarity. It wasn't until I started doing that things changed for me. I began writing and sent a story to *Chicken Soup for the Soul*. The second I received the letter of acceptance was unlike any ever before, love flooded into my heart and I knew that this was what I had to do with my life. You see though, I had to start writing to learn that my biggest passion was indeed writing. That only came with consistent action. The experience is the reward; clarity comes through the process of exploring. Action is where you get results.

2. **Drop from Your Head to Your Heart.** Your heart is your best tool to access your true purpose and passion. Ask yourself what you love? Start taking steps to do what you love. When you are inspired and connected to your happy self, inspiration floods your heart and soul. When you lead from your heart, you are naturally more joyful and motivated to explore. By doing what you love, you will be inspired and gain insights into what brings you the most joy.
3. **Break Up with the "ONE"** Many of us struggle because we try to find that ONE thing that we are meant to do; but trying to find only one thing is the reason why we feel like something is missing. The notion that we have only one thing we are meant for limits us from fulfilling our greatness. Take me for example; I have six different job titles. I'm a life coach, travel writer, author, speaker, teacher, mentor, designer, and each thing I do brings me joy, but none of these are my purpose, they are my

passions. So, start getting in touch with your passions! When you lead a passionate life you are living your life on purpose.

Let go of thinking there is only one purpose for you and embrace the idea that our purpose in life is to love life fully by putting ourselves into our life! This means we jump in and try new things; we stop resisting the unknown and we fully engage in what is happening right here, where we are. To lead a purposeful life, follow your passions. When we live a passion-filled life we are living on purpose, and that is the purpose of life. That feeling that something is missing goes away when you lead a passion-filled life. The need to seek our purpose comes from a lack of passion. When you don't feel connected to your life, you lack purpose and passion. To fix this emptiness simply add more passion. To boil it down, remember this simple equation:

Passion + Daily Action = Purposeful Life

Consider that the real purpose of anyone's life is to be fully involved in living. Try to be present for the journey and fully embrace it. Soon you will be oozing with passion, and you will feel so purposeful and fulfilled you will wonder how you lived life without it. Enjoy the journey into your own awesome life.

So, there you have it. Purpose is literally everywhere. All around you. You simply cannot avoid it. Serving our country offers you a remarkable opportunity to feel a strong connection with mission and purpose. You signed up because this all meant something to you, and that purpose likely deepened as you trained for and received your mission. You served dutifully, and your life and your purpose became entangled into one, intersecting during every moment of your life. You moved toward an objective, a specific mission with tremendous value and importance. Now you are back home, looking to replace all of that connection and meaning. It isn't easy. But it isn't impossible either.

The first step: Recognize just how important purpose is to your transition back to civilian life. The second step: Understand that missions can be different yet still have value. The final step: Work to ensure that you find purpose in your life, to hedge against the changes you are likely experiencing. As you find purpose, you will find meaning; and as you find meaning, you will find connection. Once you feel connected, you will never feel alone.

Chapter 8

ARCHITECTING A NEW FUTURE:

Discovering Dreams, Wealth, and Aspirations

This chapter is the most exciting for me to write but also one of the hardest. This is the chapter that could potentially help you truly create a new, meaningful, and incredibly rewarding life path.

Many people are never taught to think about what they really want out of life. They think about their bills, the work they're behind on, the places they need to take the kids, and a whole list of things to do to get through another day. Not many people sit down and dream about possibilities. Let's all admit it, working forty to sixty-five or eighty hours a week and just working to wait for the weekend is not a fulfilling life.

The other issue: We ask ourselves the wrong questions. When many veterans are leaving the service, they're asking what job are they going to get. Granted, we must land somewhere so the bills will be covered, but there is so much more to our lives. Money for bills is only a part of the effort. The real questions are more about what else really excites you.

No one is asking:

- "How much free time do I want?"
- "What do I want to spend money on?"
- "Who do I want to spend time with?"
- "What do I want to do for fun?"
- "Where do I want to travel?"
- "What would I do if money weren't a problem?"
- "Who would I like to help?"

Many veterans are simply working on ways of getting back to self-sufficiency. The simple act or ability to get through the day might seem as unlikely as taking a trip to the moon. And, I would add, getting veterans to this basic level is an admirable goal in the beginning.

At the same time, are coping, self-sufficiency, and "getting by" the best we should expect for ourselves and our veterans? Is that the best we're going to offer? Again, great beginnings, but life offers so much more and our veterans have it in them to reach the highest levels of happiness and success by anyone's definition. I can't imagine being satisfied with just coping or self-sufficiency for myself, and I certainly can't accept that as the new standard of care for our nation's veterans. While coping and improved living are great steps in the right direction, today's veterans should expect to be among the best, brightest, and wealthiest individuals in our country. If we don't set that as our goal as a country, we're letting hundreds of thousands of young men and women fade away—and, to an extent, just using them for our benefit in their military service and forever depleting their potential just to discard them.

As Bob Proctor says, "Most people tip-toe through life, hoping they'll make it safely to death."

This chapter provides an alternate path, a path where the reader can and should dream about what it means to have a "wonderful life." Just sustaining or maintaining is not enough. Each veteran has the key ingredient to reach some of the highest levels of achievement. That ingredient is discipline. They have that in spades.

When we enter the military, we put our civilian lives on hold. We begin our training and start to program ourselves to be very successful at our military missions. We learn to trust the people next to us, and we devote ourselves to making sure they can trust us. We become exceptionally good at what we do. We know what we're supposed to do, and we follow our training. That's what we do. During this time in the military, the thought of dreams and aspirations are not what fills our minds.

I was talking to an old-time logger about when to cut some trees down on my property. He shared with me that he'd been doing this for more than sixty years, then said, "You have to cut the right trees down and let the light come in. If you don't, your forest will just go dormant; it won't grow." It's the same for our minds. "Stuff" clutters our minds. We need to clear some of it out to make room for dreams. If we don't, we'll become stale and dormant.

This chapter serves as the next step in helping veterans see themselves in becoming more, replacing the nightmares with dreams and aspirations of what they can become and rediscovering their full potential. If veterans can achieve peak performance in their roles in the military through the knowledge, training, devotion to mission, and sheer willpower, then they can absolutely achieve that level on the civilian side of the equation.

Here's where that process begins!

Discovering Dreams

Up to this point, this book has provided ways to think after we transition to civilian life by redirecting and shifting our beliefs about ourselves, the people around us, and what we expect of our relationships. We've talked about exchanging our military tribes for new ones; we've looked at ways of shifting our mental states through forgiveness and recovery. We've looked at the science of what is happening to our minds and how we can use that knowledge to help us cope. We've learned about placing greater value on our family and friends to provide a network of people to help us and to create an environment where we're not alone. We've started to create a new identity where we see ourselves differently. At this point, we're ready for this next step, which not only allows us to catch up with society but allows us to lead. Michelangelo reminds us: "The greater danger for most of us lies not in setting our aim too high and falling short; but in setting our aim too low and achieving our mark."

I have always been impressed with how the military can train anything it sets its mind to. It can take the most mundane or complex topics and turn them into a class. And, at the end of the class you've become a master. But the military doesn't train visioning for your civilian life. It doesn't teach how to become wealthy, and it doesn't teach our veterans how to become the best entrepreneurs, manufacturing engineers, chief financial officers, chief executive officers, contract plumbers, artists, or anything like that. It simply doesn't train people to dream about their futures. At the end of a person's service, the military helps with job placement services and résumé writing and interviewing skills, but that's only the very beginning of what people need to be highly successful.

This chapter will lay out a process to help you create a completely new self-image. You deserve a wonderful, fulfilling life.

To realize your full potential, use your mind differently and ask questions you may have never spent any time thinking about. You're going to start working on answering: What do I really want to accomplish in life? What can I really accomplish? How far can I go? How far can I stretch? If I really put my mind to it, how much could I impact other people's lives? Not only will you ask these questions, but once you start, you will begin to see a very different future for yourself, your family, and others around you. Napoleon Hill said, "Whatever the mind can conceive and believe, it can achieve." Dreaming big is incredibly important to everyone. The following ten reasons show why you should dream about your future:

1. **It connects you with your inner passion, your true sense of self.** This is where the "it" happens! When you connect with what you're passionate about and drives you, you remove your self-imposed limits. Dreaming big while stirring your soul's passions naturally creates success. No matter the obstacles, you can do what you love and earn income in the process. Take the time to know what you're passionate about, write it down, and start dreaming about all the things you can do.
2. **It helps you focus on the positives instead of the negatives in life.** Life's challenges can overwhelm us. The harder the challenge, the bigger you must dream. When you have a big enough dream, you can stay focused on achieving that goal instead of all of the negativity that can swirl around you. In life, you get what you focus on. When you focus on positive outcomes, you attract more positivity into your life. Even when negative things happen, keeping a positive focus on our dreams will provide a path through the negative times. It is a very powerful aid.

3. **It gives you purpose**.

   Purpose is like the rock in our lives. It's our foundation. Life constantly changes, but having dreams that you are deeply connected with gives you the power to chase them and never give up. When you have a purpose, it exudes onto others and inspires them to find their own passions and dreams. The dreams expose your true purpose and help you see what really drives you forward.

4. **It drives you.**

   I learned this from my personal experiences. About fifteen years ago when money was very tight, I was out of cash and thought I couldn't make payroll the next day. Too many people relied on me, and I couldn't just walk away. That never even entered my mind. I sat alone in my office thinking of every possible way I could obtain the $16,000 needed for payroll. I hadn't shared this dilemma with anyone because I didn't want to worry anybody. Just then, I heard a knock on my door. Unbeknownst to me, my receptionist had talked to her husband over the weekend and decided the night before to loan the company $20,000. To say I was shocked is an understatement. The contribution was life-changing. Words could not express my gratitude. Apparently, my passion was so convincing, she had decided to contribute in an unbelievable way. Passion and drive are infectious. I never did let on how close we were to such a dire situation. Trust me, I'm not the first entrepreneur to have faced this challenge.

5. **It promotes growth and change.**

   Dreaming big helps create a new vibe in your life. The changes are obvious to others around you and will drive a new sense of self-worth. Personal growth is powerful and will change your life forever. The growth and change come from you making investments in yourself. It's all interconnected. When you have big dreams, you have drive and determination; you have a positive outlook; you start to pursue your passion; and you start to grow and change as a result.

6. **It makes you focus.**
   What you focus on, you receive! This pertains to everything in life. If you focus on the negative, you will receive more negativity; if you focus on your dreams, you will get closer to achieving those dreams. It's called the "Law of Attraction." When you reflect on your dream every day or even multiple times a day, you will constantly move yourself and your actions toward that goal. You will begin to attract things into your life that will complement your dream too. Without a dream, you lack focus; with a dream and a burning desire, you can't help but be focused.
7. **It makes it easier to take action.**
   Lacking a vision creates uncertainty. Uncertainty creates hesitance. A clear, concise dream provides clarity and purpose. Decisions become easier because you can see how there is a connection to your dream. It becomes easier and easier to take the steps and actions necessary to succeed.
8. **It creates a new reality of success in your mind.**
   By writing out your dreams, they become more tangible. Writing is incredibly powerful. The action allows your mind to start processing your dream as though it is reality. Your subconscious can't tell the difference, so it convinces your conscious of the new reality. You begin creating in reality what is only an image in your mind. Bob Proctor constantly says, "If you can create it in your mind, you can hold it in your hand."

9. **It forces you to be more creative**.
   Creativity is such an important element in a person's success. It's one of the things I try to assess in an interview with a prospective employee. Do they use their creativity? Most people lack genuine creativity when they start the dreaming process. Over time, as each person puts more emphasis on the details of their dream, it takes more and more creativity. We must use creativity to imagine a new future. The more creativity, the more clarity in our dreams, the more purpose we feel, and the greater the chances of success.
10. **It teaches your children and others that it is good to dream.**
   One of the greatest things about success? It sets an example for others to follow. Your success generates success for people around you. For me, it is the greatest gift I've found. I encouraged and allowed my children to create and pursue their dreams. I have been very fortunate in how they each created their own dreams and pursued them in spite of challenges. My daughter overcame learning disabilities and a school counselor who told her she'd never succeed in a biology career. She's now an aquatic biologist married to a landscape architect, and they are running their own successful business. My son pursued his passion for creating video and became a documentary filmmaker. He's been an on-air personality on a podcast that reaches more people than CNN and MSNBC combined; and he is about to release his first film after traveling the world to study how to redefine how education should be delivered. My adult children inspire me.

You need three things to succeed: 1) discipline, 2) a clear goal (mission, vision, purpose), and 3) courage.

The most important attribute to success is discipline. Discipline is our ability to demand something of ourselves, regardless of the consequences, and to follow through. If there is a better example of what the military has trained each and every veteran for, I don't know what it is. We may not have liked discipline because of the negative perception of the word, but everything a veteran does with success is based on discipline. Check it off the list, you've got that. The second most important element of success is having a clear, intricate image of your goal and exactly how it looks at a point in the future. If you don't know how to do that, we'll teach you. The third really important element of success is courage. Courage relies on your discipline to overcome any fear. Courage is based on the belief you have in the discipline you've achieved.

So, of the three things you need to succeed—discipline, goals, and courage—you certainly have the discipline. Most likely, you also have courage and conviction. Now, you need to develop the skills to dream and create a clear mission, vision, and purpose. Bob Proctor reminds us: "Set a goal to achieve something that is so big, so exhilarating that it excites you and scares you at the same time."

We all have senses such as taste, touch, sight, smell, and hearing. As I've heard Bob Proctor say in the past, "I have a dog that can see, smell, taste, touch, and hear. What makes us different, besides the fact that dogs can hear and smell much better than we can, is the fact that we possess other mental faculties." According to Bob, these are imagination, intuition, perception, will, memory, and reason. We must exercise these faculties.

For the most part, people used their imagination extensively when they were young. But then, society tells us to grow up and pay attention—stop daydreaming and get to work. The problem? Imagination is one of the most powerful faculties we have; it is what sets truly successful people apart from ordinary individuals. Take a moment and look around at the things of convenience that were not around five, ten, or thirty years ago—things like the internet, cell phones, Facebook, flat-screen TVs, texting, digital cameras, and many others that were once only an idea in someone's head. Now, we can barely live without these things. All of it began in the imagination of one person. It wasn't real until they created it in their mind. Once it was created in their mind, the only thing keeping it from reality was the person's strong belief in the idea and their discipline and courage to see it through.

The power of vision or imagination is inconceivable. A clear vision, backed with the courage to carry it out, significantly increases your chances of success. It's that simple. When your life is focused and filled with purpose, you are far more likely to experience fulfillment and significance.

A vision is like a mental lighthouse, a beacon to constantly draw our attention. We are naturally drawn to it like bugs to a light. The stronger the vision, the brighter the light. If we stay focused on this beacon called our vision, it will become reality. We can achieve whatever we can conceive. If we can hold it in our minds, we can hold it in our hands. So, the question becomes how do we exercise our imaginations? How do we create our visions? How do we light this beacon in our minds?

Consider seven ways to exercise your imagination:

1. **Quiet your mind.** As I mentioned earlier, you have to create space for your mind to utilize your imagination. The noise from the day or your pressures and stress will cause your creative mind to go dormant. Meditation is one good way to clear your mind. Get someplace quiet with no distractions. Sometimes, it drives my wife crazy to see me just sitting and looking outside.

The fact is, I'm not even looking at what's outside; I'm only seeing what's playing in my mind.

2. **Start to think about what you enjoy doing.** Break new ground when you do this. Don't create any boxes to live within. Look back at your life and think about what really brought you enjoyment. To that end, I've begun glassblowing. That was totally off the beaten path for me. Now, my wife has several glass pumpkins because I opened my mind to new ideas.
3. **Get on the internet, and start searching things you have an interest in.** The internet can provide a wealth of information about anything we can imagine. Just start looking at anything that piques your curiosity.
4. **Look at what other people are doing.** Watch out for how other people are chasing their dreams, and ask them how they pursue them. Remember though, you cannot copy someone else's passion. Your passion is yours and yours alone. Watch other people to stir your own imagination, to jumpstart your own creativity.
5. **Try.** Jacquelyn McKenzie is a personal and professional coach who teaches people Bob Proctor's "Thinking Into Results" and is the bestselling author of *The Prophet of Profit*. I first met Jacquelyn at a Bob Proctor event and then hired her as a coach for my senior leadership team.

I sat down with her for an interview, and she recommends: "Just trying different things that sound interesting. Don't be afraid to try a bunch of things at first. You don't know what you haven't experienced." For me, I've started growing an orchard of cherries, peaches, and pears; I started glassblowing; I travel to warm places in the winter; I started to focus on photography; I'm writing a book, and I created a foundation for veterans. I've done all of this because I wanted to test out my imagination and the bounds of my passion. I love to create things, so the question becomes: Where can I create?

1. **Write down your ideas.** Get a journal and keep notes when you exercise your imagination. Use these notes to further dream and imagine as you build upon your earlier ideas. Writing down these ideas will prevent you from just withering away. You would be surprised how much of our imaginations just drive by the front window of our minds, never to be seen again.
2. **Repeat.** Try, try, try, and then try again. Make notes, do internet research, talk to people, meditate, and think of your future. People say it takes thirty days to develop a habit. Stay on track with these simple exercises; you will exercise your imagination, replace your problems and fears with aspirations, and begin to create a new vision for yourself. Take notes, review them often, and keep dreaming!
3. **Mastermind.** One way to help with your ideas: Join or create what's called a mastermind. The mastermind is a group of success-minded people who meet face-to-face or remotely. I joined a mastermind led by Jacquelyn McKenzie to help both of us and others pursue our individual dreams. People in these groups can help you dream bigger, strive higher, and see your future more clearly. The group can be made up of whomever you want to work with.

Mastermind groups offer a combination of brainstorming, education, peer accountability, and support to focus your personal and business goals. A mastermind group helps you and the group members achieve success. Members challenge each other to set strong goals, and more importantly, to accomplish them.

The group requires commitment, confidentiality, and the willingness to give and receive advice and ideas. Its members support each other with total honesty, respect, and compassion.

From Dreams to Wealth

More than 48,000 veteran service organizations exist. Some help families financially during a loss. Some provide veterans with needed medical care. Some help veterans train animals; and many other very helpful programs exist. However, in my research, I have not found programs helping veterans become wealthy, extremely successful, or truly satisfied with their ultimate passion in life. I want to do something much more significant than just provide a hand up to help veterans become self-sufficient. I want to provide a road map of how people become successful and how that can translate into their own individual lives. This chapter aims to help veterans or their family members achieve even greater things than they ever thought possible—to dream and dream big.

There is a road map. Napoleon Hill created it after interviewing people such as Henry Ford (the inventor of mass-produced automobiles), Andrew Carnegie (the architect of the steel industry), Thomas Edison (the inventor of electricity), President Theodore Roosevelt (at forty-two years old, he is the youngest president in our country's history), and Alexander Graham Bell (the inventor of the telephone). They were the Elon Musk, Bill Gates, Jeff Bezos, and Steve Jobs of their day. From those interviews, Hill first wrote *The Laws of Success*, and then at the request of Henry Ford, he wrote a more condensed version in *Think and Grow Rich*.

In addition, Bob Proctor, author of *You Were Born Rich,* is a personal development legend in his own right. *Think and Grow Rich* originally inspired Bob, who has become a thought leader on what it takes to become wealthy and successful. Much of what I write in the next two chapters have a basis in both Hill's and Proctor's books and lessons.

One key to becoming wealthy? Develop a proper understanding of what wealth is and what it is not. This may be shocking to you, but I'll say it—money is not the goal. The accumulation of wealth by itself is not the type of wealth I'm talking about. Money provides two primary purposes: to make you comfortable and to allow you to provide service far beyond the limits of your physical presence. The driving goal of wealth is to experience the ultimate freedom of time to enjoy it.

I have realized that the most precious commodity, beyond any physical possession, is time. In one of my early business failures, I lost $1.8 million chasing an opportunity that I shouldn't have. I allowed someone to mislead me on critical information I needed to know before I spent almost two years trying to make something work. After two hard-fought years, I ended up walking away from the effort. I hold myself accountable because I should have done my own research. It was incredibly painful to lose that much money; I don't recommend it for everyone. But I learned that I could recover the money, and I did. At the same time, I will never get back the benefits we could have had from using my company's resources to aim at a different target. I will never get back the two years I wasted on this opportunity. Time is more valuable than money.

On the other side of that coin, wealth allows you to utilize your time to do the things you enjoy. For example, I don't like temperatures that begin with a minus sign. One year, the temperature in Traverse City, Michigan, was -26 degrees Fahrenheit for an entire two weeks. I told my wife that I had had enough. So, she retired a year later, and we have been spending six to eight weeks a year in warm places since then.

We've been to Hawaii for a month at a time and the Caribbean, Mexico, and the Southern US during the winter months for the last six years. That is the ultimate freedom of time: to enjoy my life traveling with my wife. I set up my business so I can run it while I travel. I have a very capable senior management team, and I can work for the most part from anywhere in the world.

Again, it's not about the money, it's about how you become wealthy and use wealth. It's not about getting to the end or just accumulating wealth—it's the journey and experiences along the way. The path to wealth and beyond is about growing personally, professionally, and financially.

Almost everyone who lacks money shares in a universal experience. Money consumes our time and our mental capacity when we don't have it. We waste tremendous energy worrying about it when we lack it. We constantly imagine all the bad things that we're convinced will happen if we don't get money. This worry is always a huge waste. It's the damaging cycle you must break out of. Wealthy people don't worry about money. This worry about the money we don't have and the time wasted on it robs people of their dreams and aspirations. It takes away the unbelievable mental power each one of us possesses.

Wealth is about the pursuit of our dreams, the ability to share what we have with others with the spirit of generosity. Wealth is not selfish and bad. It's about fulfillment and creation. Money doesn't create bad people. It only makes already bad people more obvious. On the contrary, money in the hands of generous, happy people can translate into them sharing their wealth in ways that elevate others.

People have the misconception that you must have a great deal of money to accomplish anything of significance. Not true. I've climbed the mountains of Colorado to hunt elk. If you have ever had a chance to get up in altitude where the snow line is, you'll see the slow drips of water at altitudes where the snow melts. Those drips accumulate into a puddle, then a creek, then a stream, then a river that merges with another river to become a great flow of power. These great tributaries started as a single drip. These drips have carved great valleys and canyons.

In this same way, pursuing wealth starts with a small spark of a dream. It's different for each and every single person. It's your dream, your passion, your life purpose. No one else can experience it for you and if you don't pursue it, no one will. Your inexperienced purpose will remain just that—inexperienced.

As I grew up, I dreamed and fantasized about being in a cockpit of an aircraft. I used to get flying magazines and cut out the pictures of the cockpits and planes. I wanted it bad. We would always bid on introductory flights during those public television fundraisers. It just never worked out. Fast-forward about ten years. I was walking to my class at Michigan State my senior year. As I mentioned earlier in the book, as I did, I was thinking of my dad. He had passed away two years earlier, but I could hear his voice and I remember him saying, "I always wished I would have learned how to fly." As I heard him, I looked up to find myself walking in front of the Air Force recruiting headquarters. I took a right turn, walked in, and nine months later, I was attending Officer Training School down in San Antonio, Texas. Three months later, I was in navigator training and the very first aircraft I'd ever been in, a twin-engine jet trainer T-37 with the throttle in one hand and the control stick in the other. The cockpit looked just like I imagined it, but I could not even imagine what it was like to actually fly it. It was my dream and a part of my purpose fulfilled. Wealth is not about money. As Robert Kiyosaki, author of *Rich Dad Poor Dad*, said: "Your mindset matters. If you don't have the mindset of a wealthy person ('How can

I afford it?') versus a poor person ('I can't afford it.'), you will never achieve wealth."

What Is Wealth?

So, what is wealth and what does it look like? If you really want to know what wealth looks like, look for people who have found their purpose in life. One of the best examples for me is Edward Lowe.[52] Consider this story his son said he always liked telling: In 1947, Mr. Lowe, a twenty-seven-year-old Navy veteran who had been working in his father's sawdust business, received a visit from a cat-loving Cassopolis, Michigan, neighbor whose sandbox had frozen.

She asked Mr. Lowe for some sawdust, which was most commonly used for cat litter, but on a sudden inspiration he suggested she try something he had in the trunk of his car: a bag of kiln-dried granulated clay, a highly absorbent mineral that his father, who sold sawdust to factories to sop up grease spills, had begun offering as a fireproof alternative.

She came back for more; then he began to sell the product for sixty-five cents per bag, and when customers returned asking for "Kitty Litter" by name, a business and a brand were born.

Adapting clay for use as a cat box litter made Mr. Lowe a millionaire many times over. He sold his Kitty Litter operations for $200 million (plus stock) in 1990. To help other entrepreneurs and to make sure they didn't suffer some of the same ills he experienced from his fast-won wealth, Mr. Lowe created the Edward Lowe Foundation, which sponsors a variety of programs at his 3,000-acre estate in southwestern Michigan. I've visited there. It's a fantastic place with a main lodge and outdoor walking paths through nature. Facilitators help entrepreneurs learn about leadership and

---

52 https://www.nytimes.com/1995/10/06/us/edward-lowe-dies-at-75-a-hunch-led-him-to-create-kitty-litter.html

ways to help their companies. His wealth wasn't all about the money; it circulated and is helping small business owners in Michigan.

He sold dirt, became a multimillionaire, and left a legacy of helping entrepreneurs. Now, if that story doesn't motivate you, I don't know what will.

How about Steve Jobs, who along with Steve Wozniak founded Apple at age twenty in his parents' garage? How about J.K. Rowling, who at age twenty-eight was divorced, penniless, a single mother, suffered from depression, and on government-assisted welfare? Two years later, she wrote the first of the Harry Potter series for a $2,000 advance. Then there's Debbie Fields, who at twenty years old started selling chocolate cookies with her husband. They built the $450 million cookie business named Mrs. Fields.

We see these people after they've generated wealth and think it's unobtainable. That's just not true. Each and every one of them dealt with adversity, lacked funding, and had no real experience in business. They all reached financial wealth, but it was the discovery of their passion and the pursuit of it that was the wealth.

What do wealthy people do with their money? According to the "2018 US Trust Survey of High-Net-Worth People," wealthy people share a common trait of giving back to society. Ninety percent give charitably compared to just 56 percent of the general population, and they donate on average ten times the amount. They're also charitable with their time. Forty-nine percent of high-net-worth people donate their time to charitable activities. They find a way to contribute to others, which is counter to the stereotype so often attributed to the wealthy. Wealth is not about accumulation; it is about circulation.

Charles Schwab surveyed 1,000 Americans as part of an annual "Wealth Index." The top seven items that people listed when it comes to a rich daily life were spending time with family (62 percent), taking time for themselves (55 percent), owning a home (49 percent), meals out or delivered (41 percent), subscription services like Netflix (33 percent), grooming and pampering (29 percent), and having the latest tech gadgets (27 percent). All other items were below 25 percent of respondents, including having a busy social life and a bunch of specific examples of spending.

It's worth noting that the top two responses have very little to do with money at all.

Wealth to me personally is my ability to spend my time the way I want to. It's about getting to see my grandchildren and walking through my property with my wife. It's about cutting wood, building a fire pit, or going to glassblowing classes. It's about pursuing my faith. It's about going on mission trips to Africa or Honduras. It's about donating my time to help at my church. It's the freedom to not worry about debt and the ill effects of the weight of financial stress. It's about my ability to create businesses and wealth for all my employees and a foundation for veterans where we can mentor them and help them become as wealthy and successful as they define that to be.

The point of this discussion? There is no one image of wealth. The image is different for every person. It involves pursuing their passion, spending more time with their family and friends, and using their time more in the way each person wants to, which is often toward charitable activities. When you create the image of wealth in your mind, it is yours to create. Feel free to start with the laundry list: the big boat, the larger house, the vacations, the nicer cars, the toys like jet skis or four-wheelers, and all the other luxury items. Chances are, you'll start to think of other ways you want to spend your money and time. You'll start to think of other people and how you can help meet their needs.

Generosity of spirit is the openness and willingness to share our own "gifts" freely with others, joyously and willingly, without expectation of receiving anything in return. Generosity of spirit is created through respect and compassion for others; it involves experiencing and celebrating what is important to another person.

When we share in this way, we generate abundance and increase prosperity for all. This helps us make a difference and transform other people's lives; generate creative, innovative solutions; lead by example; strengthen our acceptance of responsibility and that of others; share our wisdom and knowledge for everyone's benefit; explore and build connecting threads where none previously existed, and foster peace and harmony. We can celebrate all that becomes possible as a result.

The Value of Aspirations in Action

I spoke with a Vietnam War veteran named Gordon Oosting. He shared a story of his last day in combat. He was at the front line in a firefight with the enemy. The fighting was intense and casualties resulted on both sides of the battle. A lull occurred in the fighting, and he was sent back to the forward operating base (FOB) and told he was headed home. Several hours later, he was on an aircraft heading to the US. Less than twenty-four hours later, he was in the States and making his way back to Grand Rapids, Michigan. Bam! He was out, done, and back to the civilian world in less than twenty-four hours after shooting at the enemy. Now what? There was no preparation, long drawn-out redeployment, or mind-numbing out-processing scenario. He was out!

Well, life wasn't over, and he had to figure it out. Gordon was lucky. He had friends and relationships to help him transition. He told me how bizarre it was though when he first returned. There was no warming up or down depending how you want to look at it. But he managed. Some did, and some did not. Just like today, some do, and some don't transition easily.

Life does not end after service. Your purpose doesn't end. Your mission doesn't end. It must not end, but it does need to start over. For many who struggle in their transition, it doesn't feel like much of a transition at all. The most common emotion is being overwhelmed. Techniques outlined earlier in this book should provide some understanding and steps to help reduce the struggle if even only somewhat. Knowledge is power.

So, how do we move from overwhelmed to being invigorated by new possibilities? First, start with a belief that there *is* a new possibility. No matter what, convince yourself that a new, even brighter possibility exists. Use as many of the techniques in this book to calm your mind and become open to new prospects. Then, start to use some of the ideas in this chapter on using your imagination to create images of this new direction.

1. Quiet your mind.
2. Think about what you enjoy, where you are talented.
3. Do some research.
4. Look around and see what others are doing; you may imitate, but don't just settle for someone else's dreams.
5. Try different things, experiment, ask a ton of questions.
6. Write down your thoughts and ideas all along the way.
7. Repeat over and over.

It won't happen overnight, but you will begin dreaming of your new purpose and new mission. You must replace thoughts of being overwhelmed with thoughts of excitement about things you enjoy doing;

and you must understand that you can start to do those things. You must believe that 100 percent.

Look, if a former Navy guy can package dirt to become wealthy, anything is possible. That thought alone should motivate you.

The deeper the void you feel after leaving your military service or the greater your sense of feeling lost, the bigger your dreams need to be. You can't sit on the sidelines and watch the game of life. Whatever hole you feel you are in will only get deeper. The only way out is to dream and dream big.

Bob Proctor divides goals into three types:[53] A, B and C goals. An "A" goal is a goal that you know how to do. For example, if you have a goal to buy a new car, but you have experience in the past of buying a new car, that's an "A" goal since you know how to do it. It doesn't challenge you or help you grow because you already know how to do it.

A "B" goal is something you haven't done before, but you have confidence that you can get it done. Consider this example of when I started planting fruit trees in front of my property: Growing fruit trees was a new experience, and I knew that I'd need to learn some things, but they were trees. I could learn about the specifics of growing fruit trees and how to get them to produce great fruit. I had a pretty good idea of how to do this.

A "C" goal is something that you really want ... something that really inspires you; but it scares you too. In the current moment, a "C" goal might seem like a fantasy. Most people, when they contemplate their "C" goal, quickly brush it aside and never pursue it because of fear or not believing they can achieve it. Going after a "C" goal may require something "drastic" like quitting your job, borrowing a large sum of money, writing this book, moving to another city, or getting

---

53 https://www.linkedin.com/pulse/what-difference-between-goal-b-c-matthew-t-ray

out of a relationship. It's moving out of your comfort zone and heading straight for, what Bob Proctor calls, the "Terror Barrier." But if you break through the Terror Barrier, growth and inspiration await. You don't have to know exactly how you will reach your "C" goal; you just have to decide to do it and start moving toward it. The universe will guide you if you believe you can.

Orville and Wilbur Wright's decision to build an aircraft would be considered a C goal. But a C goal is individual. It doesn't need to change the world; it only needs to change and inspire the person who sets it. When I decided to start the Patriot Promise Foundation to create an enterprise for veterans to not only find work but to develop the skills necessary to achieve their full potential and to find their true passions, that was taking a C goal to the next level. It's not only a C goal, but it's meaningful to me. These goals are exciting and scary at the same time.

Come up with ideas and goals that excite you and scare you at the same time. You might wonder if you're nuts just for thinking about it, or maybe you can't figure out exactly what to do. That's okay because it's not important to know all the answers at the beginning. Your passion, energy, and drive will keep you on a path toward your vision.

Chapter 9

FROM SERVICE TO SUCCESS:

Recognizing Key Strengths to Thrive

As I begin this closing chapter, I want to reflect on what I set out to do when I began writing this book. I wanted to share my own challenges, not to draw attention to myself; to help readers understand that I personally relate to some of the challenges veterans face; to provide pertinent research to allow readers to understand some of the deeper aspects of what they may be encountering; and to provide a platform for other veterans to share their personal transition experiences in hopes that their voices would carry weight in delivering some of the important messages. I also wanted to provide specific steps veterans can take not only to become self-sufficient but to reach beyond current limits and achieve some of the highest levels of success and wealth. And, most of all, I wanted readers to believe that an even brighter future lies ahead of them if they choose to focus on creating it.

I systematically reviewed each chapter to provide a bit of a review and to help the reader navigate the information, advice, and tips for finding their new future. The title of the book, *From Service to Success: New Mission, New Purpose, and a New Journey to a Great Life*, promises that this book is about a transition and change. In fact, it's a massive change physically, mentally, spiritually, and in just about every possible aspect of a veteran's life and the lives of their families and friends. The change is going to happen, so the hope of this book is to put the veteran and their family in the driver's seat of change instead of being changed by circumstances.

Your Journey Begins NOW!

The first proactive change is to understand a few things and reflect on what has helped you arrive here. The first chapter asked you to assess why you or your loved one joined the military, to understand that there was a higher calling in most cases. Each veteran did not perform a solo role in the military; they were part of a greater team and should not expect to be on their own once they leave. Your military buddies might not be next to you, but that doesn't mean you're alone. Transitioning will not happen overnight; it will take a village, and it will require changes in attitude toward finding a new purpose. If you feel you need help, seek it. If you recognize that someone else needs help, work with them to seek it. If someone points you in the direction of seeking help, please don't ignore them. Most importantly, remember that you are not alone. People care, and throughout the process, there is hope.

The second chapter begins to highlight the reasons the people around us are so important. We are tribal in our habits. We need to belong and feel needed and connected. That was important during our service, and it remains true afterward. The problem? We have trouble seeing our new civilian tribe for who they are. That's why practicing gratitude is so incredibly important. Not only is the practice enormously helpful in shifting our attitudes toward the positive, it opens our minds to different possibilities too. Its importance is why I introduced this as the first new behavior to practice. Writing down things we are grateful for causes the mind to become more grateful and opens our eyes to things we may not have seen. It's a practice as important as push-ups or sit-ups are for physical conditioning. Each and every veteran must trade in what they appreciated in their service and become open to new possibilities in their civilian worlds.

Many veterans have sacrificed far more than I have in my service. They bring back much greater challenges than I can imagine. In fact, many bring back things almost too great to bear. The third chapter reminds you that you're healing. The mental aspects are as critical and important as any physical injuries. One of the most important mental conditions to treat is the guilt that many carry home. Forgiveness is not just a simple phrase like "I'm sorry" or "I forgive you." It is a process of stopping an invisible enemy from keeping you from your future. Self-forgiveness is high on the list of importance and is as crucial as a cast is for a broken arm. Additionally, start to make some decisions that recognize the healing process and the steps needed to build a healthier you.

Some forces are at play in our minds that we probably have not been fully aware of. In Chapter 4, I've tried to bring in some education about the mind versus the brain or our physical being. We need to understand that we as veterans were programmed to our mission and military purpose. The term "paradigm" is fundamental to our understanding. We must start creating brand-new paradigms and programming our subconscious minds in a way that will lead us beyond our military pasts. Remember that the subconscious doesn't select what is true or not.

Sometimes, that works against us, but we can use it to our advantage too. If we constantly put positive information into our subconscious minds, then ultimately, we will generate positive results. That's a fact.

While the mind is a powerful tool, we cannot ignore our bodies. While the military was preparing our minds with new paradigms and reshaping our purpose, it was also honing our physical well-being. Just because we leave the military doesn't mean we should give up on the habits we used to keep in physical shape. Chapter 5 presents information about how the brain contributes to our maintenance of well-being. Neurochemicals produced in the brain can help create a better sense of happiness and enjoyment. Many of these neurochemicals are created and positively impacted by physical activity and healthy actions. Sleep is most important for our well-being. If there is one thing that can help you and other veterans, it is establishing good sleep habits. If you or someone you know is struggling with their sleep, seek immediate help. Remember this simple equation:

Wellness: Exercise + Eating Right + Sleep = Health

While the book touches on our tribal nature earlier, Chapter 6 aims to deepen the discussion on the importance of family and friends. While the phrase, "They just don't get it" is very common, we can't just stop there. We must help our family and friends understand the common experiences veterans share as they transition into their civilian lives. Knowledge is power. By leaning on our friends and family, we can use them as sounding boards for where we might be struggling. Don't play the macho "I'll take care of it myself" type. The people we surround ourselves with after our service can be our biggest assets as we start our transitions.

Everything in the book before Chapter 7 is in preparation for the next several chapters. You've been laying the groundwork to generate a new path forward. The discovery of your new mission and purpose will determine your level of joy and contentment from this point on. So, how exactly do you discover a new mission and new purpose? The first step is to start. I've always pointed out how hard it is to learn how to swim from sitting or standing on the dock. Sometimes, you just have to jump in. That's the point with this process. You simply have to start doing things to expose those elements of life where you find your passion. This chapter provides some exercises that have led many people to find their passion. If you set the time aside and begin to watch for things and listen to what's going on around you, you can put together a picture of what excites you about living. I implore you to dedicate yourself to these efforts. Keep a journal of your ideas because while they all seem obvious and important at the time, even the greatest of all ideas can fade quickly away.

Your Interests Draw Your Attention—That Sets up Expectations—Which Creates a Burning Desire

Ready, fire, aim?! That's probably true in most people's lives. Not that it's the best process, but we've all taken a shot at things before we've had a real thought of our aim. Chapter 8 helps us understand what's involved with taking a little time to aim. My greatest hope is that even one person will take some of this book to heart and not only find a path forward but will use this information as even a small part in becoming highly successful (and even highly wealthy). It's not selfish to seek wealth as defined earlier in this book because wealth is a tool to create happiness for yourself and others. A higher calling exists other than just the gathering of money. In fact, if it's the accumulation of money you're seeking, that's not wealth. Wealth is the circulation of money. Please take the time to dream of a future. Dream about what success truly is for you. Set a goal, envision it, and add the discipline to the courage you already have—and those good things will come into being. Please use the tools in Chapter 8 to reignite the imagination within you because that is what you need in order to see yourself in "Your Future."

Finding Your Key Strengths

As you begin to move forward, as in any process, you must understand where you are before you start. To better understand where you are, do a basic self-evaluation. This self-evaluation may be a little trickier for veterans for several reasons. First, veterans aren't necessarily aware of all the strengths they carry around with them and how valuable they are to the civilian world. Secondly, veterans as a group tend to be somewhat humble. You've heard veterans say, "I was just doing my job," or "I was just doing what I'm trained to do." Quiet humility is not the name of the game in your new career path. You need to be bold, confident, and self-aware of who you are and the strengths you bring to the table.

Another reason veterans are cautious to brag or highlight their own strengths is because they know other veterans will be around to keep them in check, maybe even knock them down a peg or two. Ask a group of veterans to give you some positive feedback, and you may not get the desired outcome. I remember getting the first six-week peer evaluations from my fellow officer trainees at Officer Training School at Lackland AFB in 1987. These were affectionately called "Peer Smears." You can probably guess why. If anything, they helped me listen to how others reacted to my comments and behaviors, but they didn't build my self-image by any means. As I mentioned earlier, one of the mottos we used was, “Got a scab, we’ll pick it.” Asking fellow veterans about your strengths is not the path I would choose for this exercise.

While you don’t necessarily want to be put in your place, you do want to be honest with yourself while you focus on the positives. This section spends some time with this part of the process. Within your military experience you brought some of your personal strengths. The military probably helped you hone some new ones and strengthen ones you already possessed. As veterans, we all have a set of strengths that are incredibly important to our futures. You have within you the raw materials to begin a brand-new process to achieve your success. You will need to go through a process to discover some of these strengths, but they are there.

As I look back at my military career for my strengths, I would say I was action oriented. I always wanted to keep the ball moving forward; I didn’t need a whole lot of prodding to get things done. Learning became my strength, and I found I could consume new information quickly and ramp up on new skills pretty fast. As a navigator, I needed to communicate succinctly and clearly; at most times of a mission, success depended on it. I was responsible for making sure not only that the aircraft was on time whenever and wherever it needed to be but for pacing the crew too. I made sure checklists were run on time and that everyone was on the same page for particular parts of the mission. That all took critical communication and planning skills.

Especially important to me was that I could be trusted. That aspect probably has the deepest personal meaning to me. I did what I said I would do. I did my job at the highest level possible, and I could be counted on in the most challenging circumstances. In my mind, I had to be the best at what I did. Whether I was the navigator or the radar navigator of the B-52, I wanted my crew to feel like they had the best person in the job. To be the best, I had to know everything about the offensive aspect of the aircraft, the navigational systems, the weapons, the regulations, and the art and science of navigation. All of it. I wanted to be trusted to do all of that.

To be at the highest level, I wanted to be a part of a standardization/evaluation (Stan Eval) crew. These were the highest performing crews at a base. Early in my time on base, I approached Lt. Col. Dean, the deputy in charge of operations, to ask him what it would take and I told him that I was willing to do the things to be prepared for the job. Within a year, I became an instructor navigator and he appointed me to one of the Stan Eval crews. I set a goal and did the work, and with the help of Lt. Col. Dean, I was rewarded with the assignment. This role solidified in my mind that I could use my strengths to set similarly high goals, keep holding myself to very high standards, and achieve my goals.

The other element of my strengths has been my ability to overcome adversity. I can be persistent as a honey badger when it comes to accomplishing something. I can also take a "punch" and get back up. When my dad died from Lou Gehrig's disease (ALS), it knocked me down just like a punch in the gut. To be only nine years old when he first became sick and to experience his decline until he died when I was twenty-one was tough. It challenged my faith and understanding of fairness, and it altered my desire to become the best version of myself. It took some time for me to realize it, but his personal challenge and how he dealt with his illness and mortality left me with something powerful. My dad instilled in me a strong sense of overcoming adversity. It's etched in my soul and guides me when things don't happen the way I think they should. This strength has served me well because things normally don't go the way I think they should go. That has never stopped me though from creating even better outcomes from those situations.

Each one of us must evaluate our strengths. We need to look through periods of our lives and distill from them what makes us tick. How do we excel? Why do we accomplish great things?

Let me provide a little template that will help you evaluate yourself. The next few paragraphs will provide seven principles that are strengths any company would love every employee to have. They also happen to be the primary principles drilled into every veteran. Let me explain.

Since leaving the military and as I've grown as the owner of my business, I have dedicated much of my studies to the topic of great leadership. It's one of the pillars of my company's culture: "Dedication to providing Great Leadership to everyone who works at this company." I don't think of myself as a great leader, but I am a student of it, and I expect all my employees to be the same. Some people believe that leadership falls only on the top of the organization or on middle management. That's a load of crap. Everyone has a role in leadership and as importantly, everyone has a role in followership.

I don't care what rank you attain in the military, you are beholden to someone at a higher level. If you were enlisted, you reported to the first sergeant or another NCO. The most senior NCO reported to an officer in the unit. An O-6, captain or colonel, reported to a rear admiral or brigadier general. Even the General of the Army or Air Force reports to the President. My point? Everyone in the military must learn how to follow. Following is a key part of leadership.

Don Mercer wrote a book called *Follow to Lead*. In it, Mercer points out that following to lead is just as critical to leadership as having all eyes on the head person in charge. It's not surprising that he understands this because Mercer is a former US Army intelligence officer and CIA operations officer. As you start your civilian career, you must understand this most critical point.

According to Mercer, seven principles are required to be a great follower:

1. **Instant Response:** Begin assigned tasks immediately, complete tasks quickly. Mercer uses an example of a paratrooper: "Stand up … Hook up … Check equipment … Sound off for equipment check … stand by." When the command is made to "GO! GO! GO!" there's no hesitation. It's go time. You can probably think of a hundred examples where taking immediate action was necessary.
2. **Initiative:** People who take initiative to solve a company's problems excel above people who await orders.
3. **Imagination:** Anyone who says, "I don't have a very good imagination," is only admitting that they haven't exercised it in a long time. Trust me, it's there; it's innate in every human.
4. **Integrity:** Gain someone's trust, and you will be trusted with more. Honesty is a nonnegotiable trait.
5. **Inquire:** I call this intellectual curiosity. Ask about the what, why, who, when, and how of situations. People who understand the underlying reasons for doing things can accomplish them faster and with better outcomes.
6. **Inform:** Keeping your leader informed is always critical, but sharing information with your team helps challenge your thinking and improves how you relate to the rest of the team.
7. **Involve:** Success is a team effort. Join, participate, and ask others to join you.

It just so happens that these seven principles are critical to every employee's success in any given job. Every veteran who has received high-level training knows each one of these principles.

As you conduct your own self-assessment, use these principles as a guide. It's much more important for you to relate to these principles than for you to explain the intricacies of a 50-cal M2, M3, M107 or whatever the weapon was. Employers don't need to know the exact communications equipment you've used or how many 1,000-pound bombs I dropped on an enemy target. What they want to know is:

- Your ability to Instantly Respond means you'll take whatever training you receive and the right action without delay. You'll help others around you do the same thing. Owners like action-oriented people.
- You will take the Initiative to get the right things done, no matter the obstacle.
- You can use your Imagination to be creative in problem-solving. This has helped you keep projects on time.
- You're a person of the highest Integrity, with examples of how it's helped you become a better person.
- Your eagerness to learn and willingness to ask questions (Inquire) is solid. You're curious about how things work, and you're willing to put in extra time to learn about things outside your direct responsibilities so you can cross-train.
- You are the type of person who keeps the right people up to date and Informed. You don't wait too long to share challenges, and you make sure that ego is not going to hold anything back.
- You love teams. In fact, you can't wait to be a part of a team that is helping drive important outcomes for the company. You will Involve yourself in a team atmosphere. You can share numerous examples of teams you've led or helped elevate or when you improved their outcomes.

Create a list of examples that are personal to you. Take a hard look at some of the best work you've done, and compare it to the seven principles Mercer outlined. Your self-analysis should take a look at your personal strengths and be put into words that the civilians you're going to be speaking with can understand.

Several good tools can help you evaluate your strengths from various perspectives. Some are free and can provide a decent insight into your strong personality traits. One of the free tools I've tried is the VIA tool: https://www.viacharacter.org/. The VIA is a character strengths survey. It is free and takes about fifteen to twenty minutes to complete. It will give you some basic insight into your own personal character strengths.

Another one that I believe is highly beneficial is found in a book titled *StrengthsFinder 2.0* by Tom Rath. The book costs around $17 and comes with a coupon to take the StrengthsFinder 2.0 test, which provides you with an assessment of thirty-four characteristics. It's highly recognized and can help you understand the way commercial industry looks at these different traits. I would strongly recommend reading this book and taking the test as a part of your self-evaluation. Learn more at https://www.gallup.com/home.aspx.

Make the Right Choice

Do a Google search for "opportunities for veterans," and hundreds and hundreds of potential job opportunities for veterans will pop up. There is an unbelievable amount of assistance out there for finding a job. Even in these times of COVID-19, if you're willing to relocate and do a good job of preparing yourself, you will find employment. So, this book isn't really about being a jobs guide.

I can help give some perspective from the point of view of a CEO and what I believe is important to just about every company large or small. When I left active duty, I was told not to expect any opportunities and to receive a very low salary. Don't listen to any of that. It all comes down to how well you research opportunities, prepare for interviews, and use many networks of people to connect to your future job. Focus your time strictly in areas highlighted for veterans, but keep an open mind and look across all possible opportunities.

As CEO of my company and in my leadership positions leading up to what I do today, I have interviewed hundreds of people. Over time, I've established a pretty simple way of conducting my interviews. I start them all the same way. I try to put the interviewee at ease and let them know we're going to have a casual conversation. I'm not trying to trick them, and I'm not trying to dig into any "gotcha" kind of questions and answers. The goal of the interview is twofold. I want to know if they are a good fit for my company, and I want them to walk away able to determine if we're a good fit for them. I don't want them to interview for a job. I want them to help me decide along with them if this would be the best place for them to land where they can fulfill their highest passions.

I mean this in all sincerity. I want to find a match where they fit, where they'll love coming to work, develop into a great employee, and feel great about the decision they made. I also want my other employees to feel like I did a great job of finding them awesome teammates. I generally do not look for a particular set of skills. I look for potential. I judge potential based on drive, intellectual curiosity, values, self-directed initiative, creative problem-solving, communication, personal chemistry, and a person's ability to grow. If you look, these traits are very closely tied to what Mercer provided in his seven principles.

I based my company on this philosophy. I determined that if I built a great company culture and hired highly talented (high potential) people, it didn't matter what we were trying to do—we could excel at anything.

Potential for me is far more important than any particular skill set. Why? Because great and talented people will succeed at almost anything they tackle. They won't let any obstacle stand in their way of becoming successful. I believe that almost every veteran has that potential if they set their mind to it.

When people ask for my advice about how to prepare for an interview, what company to work for, or what to look for in a potential company, I tell them this: They need to find a company that closely matches who they are and their strengths and where they believe they can reach their full potential. How do you figure that out? Do the research. The internet provides all kinds of research resources. Look at Facebook, LinkedIn, Google searches, news articles, etc. Try to learn what the company's culture is like (if they have one). Look for a company and position that matches your strengths and passions.

You'll need to decide if you want to start your own company or work at a small company or a large company. If you decide to start your own company, this could be your best path to pursuing your passion. Many resources are available to help you start a business. It could be a franchise. Many franchises are aimed at veteran owners. Consult resources such as the Service Core of Retire Executives (SCORE), an organization of retired CEOs and executives who will offer guidance. Look to your local chamber of commerce or other local business development entities. Entire books are dedicated to helping people start their own businesses. Do not let anyone tell you that you can't do it. As a matter of fact, that is the best motivator in the world for me. Please, just tell me I can't do something.

At a small company, you'll be asked to do more and different things. Your job description will be almost constantly in flux. Relationships with coworkers can be deeper and more reliant on each other. In a large business, you will probably have more consistency. You will follow a more predictable path through the organization. Responsibilities and job titles will be more formal. Relationships will depend more on your particular department. There is no right or wrong answer. It depends on you and what you feel matches who you want to become.

So, what should you avoid? Stay away from a job that you don't feel is a match. Try not to look for a job but instead look for a match. Look for signs of poor company culture. You can get a vibe from the people you encounter. Are they passionate and happy or just overworked? Do they make positive eye contact or do they give you the stink eye? Can you see yourself hanging out with these people? The answer better be yes because you're going to spend more time with them than anyone at home. Avoid companies that do not develop their employees. Please don't work for an organization where people are not highly valued.

The most important aspect of this whole process is in preparation. Learn all you can about the companies that are hiring and the people with whom you'll be interviewing. Then, be highly prepared for your interview. I personally like the book *Knock 'em Dead: With Great Answers to Tough Interview Questions* by Martin John Yate. It does a great job to help you understand the whole interviewing process and how to best prepare for it. You'll learn how to handle some tough questions, but you'll also be very organized in reviewing your strengths and positioning them in any of your answers.

Another important aspect of the interview is asking questions. Sometimes, I get frustrated when I ask people if they have any questions for me and they say, "No, not really." I feel like, *Hey, I'm the owner of the company and I'm giving you a chance to ask me anything. Don't you want to know about the culture of the company, what's important to me, what kinds of things we do together as a company? Nothing?!*

Your questions almost say more about you than your answers. It tells your potential employer about your preparation and what's important to you, and it helps them understand if good personal chemistry exists between the two of you.

From Service to Success

Thucydides was one of the greatest ancient historians who lived (c. 460 and c. 400 BC). He wrote of war, the costs of war, and the politics of war. He wrote about it as he experienced it in his trials, failures, and successes. He served as a general for the Greek military in their war against Sparta. He knew of what he wrote. As Thucydides said, "The **Bravest** are surely those who have the clearest vision of what is before them, glory and danger alike and yet notwithstanding go out and meet it."

Now, Thucydides may have meant his comments to be directed at the glory and danger of war, but his words go so far beyond the confines of war. It takes bravery to fight America's wars. Many have given the last full measure without hesitation. Many have fought those wars and survived those sacrifices to return to a society they no longer know.

While we all know it takes bravery and courage to fight and win, it also takes bravery and courage to survive. You need to reach inside yourself to find the courage, bravery, discipline, dedication, honor, and every positive thing you picked up while in your service to forge ahead.

If we take Thucydides at his words, each returning veteran needs to find the clearest vision of what lies ahead of them, the glory and the danger, and go out and meet it. You each have within you the raw materials to not only survive but to become highly successful and wealthy in however you define success and wealth.

Everything you've experienced has made an imprint somewhere within you just as clearly as a tattoo on the surface of your skin. The scars, mental and physical, have underpinned a stronger version of yourself. The door that is closing on your military time has opened the door to a new opportunity with a new mission and new purpose for your life. Some look at these opportunities with hope and enthusiasm, and some see it in images of fear and loathing. You have choices to make, so why not choose to:

- Believe in yourself, as much as others believe in you.
- Care about those around you as though you would be going into battle with them.
- Forgive and let go of the hardest things to forgive and let go of.
- Imagine a great future, beyond what you think is possible.
- Try new experiences just because you do not know where your true passion lies.
- Love your life, even on the days it does not love you back.
- Dream not about the past but about the future where you are happy, joyful, and successful.
- Pay attention to what you think about and more attention to what is good around you.
- Give your time to finding and living your passions.
- Help other veterans and the people around you become better versions of themselves.

I'm pretty sure not many people reading this book are interested in pursuing a Miss USA crown. I think we can all agree that it's a very lofty goal. I recently read this story about Deshauna Barber and was amazed by how she overcame her own adversity from her youth, served in the military, pursued an incredibly difficult goal, and then chose to serve her fellow veterans. I would love to work with her in support of my Patriot Promise Foundation. She exemplifies everything each veteran has inside of them to set high goals, work toward them, and never give up.

Deshauna Barber graduated from Virginia State in 2015 and was the first soldier to earn the Miss USA crown. At the time of her victory, she was a logistics commander for the 988th Quartermaster Detachment Unit of the United States Army in Fort Meade, Maryland, as well as an IT analyst for the United States Department of Commerce. Barber's mother and father both served in the military, and she joined the US Army Reserve when she was seventeen.

A few years ago, when Barber sat at her own commencement at University of Maryland University College (UMUC) to secure a masters of science degree in management, she was only two weeks away from competing for a dream that took seven years and many rejections to realize: Miss USA.

Barber didn't seek pageants on her own. In 2009, during her summer break from her undergraduate studies, she was approached by a woman who thought she had a good chance of becoming Miss USA. Initially, Barber was incredulous. "I'm in the army—we don't do pageants," she said. However, once Barber learned more about the opportunity and the platform it provided, she decided to pursue it.[54]

What follows is an excerpt of her commencement speech.[55]

BARBER: And she says the most offensive things to me that you can say to a person of color in the United States of America, she asked me, "Were you born in this country?" And I was immediately offended.

---

54 https://alumni.umgc.edu/s/710/alumni/indexSocial.aspx?sid=710&gid=1&pgid=1347&cid=2767&ecid=2767&crid=0&calpgid=930&calcid=2258

55 https://speakola.com/grad/deshauna-barber-dont-fear-failure-virginia-state-2018

I put my hands on my hips and I said, "Yeah, I was born in this country." She then goes on to ask me, "How old are you?" I said, "19 years old." She says, "Are you married?" I said, "No, ma'am." She says, "Do you have any kids?" I said, "No, ma'am. May I help you find something?" She then goes on to tell me something that changed my life forever. She says, "You look like you could be the next Miss USA." And I laughed at this woman hysterically. I said, "Lady, I don't know what you're talking about. I'm going into my sophomore year at Virginia State. I'm about to commission in three years, go on active duty, be a military officer."

Somehow this crazy woman convinced me to meet her at Starbucks the very next day. She brought this foot-tall stack of pageant books and she goes on to convince me to compete in my very first pageant. I compete in my first pageant three months later and I lose.

I go back the second year, compete in my state pageant and I lose. I go back the third year, compete in my state pageant and I lose. Go back the fourth year, compete in my state pageant and lose. Go back the fifth year, compete in my state pageant and lose. But guess what happens the sixth year. I lose.

I called her on the phone six years after our Target conversation and I said, "You told me I could be the next Miss USA." And she says, "Deshauna, keep trying, keep trying, keep trying."

In June of 2015, this amazing kind of coocoo woman passes away from leukemia. In December 2015, I win Miss District of Columbia USA. In June 2016, I'm crowned the first soldier to win Miss USA. And last January in Manila, Philippines, I walked the Miss Universe stage in place top nine amongst 86.

Do not fear failure, but please be terrified of regret. When you walk out this door into the real world, you'll receive a lot of shut doors, a lot of turndown applications. You'll hear way more no's than you hear yeses.

Giving up is something I did a lot of growing up and I don't think I really challenged myself to stick anything through until I joined the track team in middle school. I remember having to ask my mom after tryouts and making it to the team for my very first pair of track shoes. Now at the time, she walks into our house and she has a bag that has a nice Nike check sign on it. So I get excited because I wasn't getting new shoes very often. I go to take the shoebox out the bag, and I noticed that it says a size nine on it. Mind you, in the seventh grade, I was a size five. I opened the box and I slide my feet into the shoe and I look at my mother and I said, "These shoes are too big." She says, "I know I did that on purpose." I was like, "Why would you buy shoes that are too big on purpose, mom?" And she says, "Because I know that you're going to grow into them."

Coach has us line up on the starting line and he wants us to run a lap around the track. As we go to take off, I immediately fall to the ground, twist my ankle because the shoes are entirely too big. See, I couldn't run at the speed that I wanted to because I didn't fit the shoes I was wearing at the time.

Now, many of us have goals we're trying to achieve, but the person we are right now is not the person that we need to be when we cross the finish line to our dreams. So, we must walk and pace ourselves on this journey to our goals because we haven't grown enough in ourselves to fit the shoes that we need to achieve our aspirations. But let me tell you something. If I had won Miss USA, my very first year, I would not have been Miss USA. I would not have been the version of myself that I needed to be to properly handle a national title.

Many of us aren't ready to walk the race. But understand that as we walk this race, we pace ourselves and as we pace ourselves, we grow, and as we grow, our foot gets bigger, and as our foot gets bigger, our shoes begin to fill. As our shoes begin to fill, we can now run a little bit faster and as we pick up the pace, we get to the finish line at the exact time we are destined to cross it.

Do not fear the word no, but be afraid of the possibility of a yes that you have prematurely destroyed because you decided to quit before the clock strikes 12. There are a lot of questions that is going to keep you up at night, but I guarantee there isn't one question that will keep you up longer at night than the question, "What if I didn't give up?"

Barber now has a powerful platform to make a difference because she would not accept "no." During her year-long tenure as Miss USA, she partnered with organizations that support military personnel and veterans. She has been a tireless advocate for soldiers suffering from post-traumatic stress disorder. As a full-time motivational speaker, she traveled the world discussing mental illness in the military, child abuse, diversity and inclusion—and the importance of being a fearless dream chaser. She continues to be an Army Reserve captain. She is now the CEO of Service Women's Action Network (SWAN), an advocacy non-governmental organization (NGO) on women soldiers and veterans. She also teaches at Howard University.

Barber hopes her story will motivate others to relentlessly pursue their goals. "Today I challenge you to fight, to work, to not stop here, to believe so heavily in your aspirations that you too will not fear the word no, but instead you will choose to welcome it."

Thank You for Your Service

I'm sure every author hopes their books are fully read, understood, and followed. I sincerely hope veterans who struggle can take the contents of this book to heart. I hope the families and friends of veterans can better understand where their loved one is coming from and perhaps pick up some ideas on how to help. At the same time, I want every reader to firmly grasp this one thing:

There is nothing in this world that a dedicated veteran cannot accomplish with the training, support, positive attitude, and discipline provided to him or her during their military training. Nothing! That means there is no settling for the minimum. There is no tapping out. There is no "going it alone." We are all part of this great big tribe called the military. It is branded on us and we can wear it with honor, rely on others around us, and help each and every veteran succeed.

If this book doesn't speak to you, get another one. If my words don't inspire action, look elsewhere. Don't stop trying to reach greatness. You have to determine what greatness and success mean to you. Most people consider success in terms of prosperity, possessions, attainment of personal hopes, and fulfillment of their true desires. But we should look beyond ourselves. Look for greater good. Raymond Holliwell, author of *Working with the Law*, said, "True genuine success of the largest kind lies in the results obtained, harvest reaped and distributed, so that our fellow beings at large are benefited, and the world enriched."

Lastly, remember that we used bravery and courage to overcome fear in combat. Fear will most assuredly confront you as you work to discover your new mission and purpose. I have no doubt about that. You will need every ounce of that bravery and courage to overcome those fears—the fear when someone tells you that you can't, or when someone ridicules your dreams, or when you allow your thoughts to be filled with self-doubt. Those are expected.

In the face of fear, you overcome it. In the face of adversity, you value and learn from it. In the face of obstacles, you go around them.

Most of all, be grateful for what you have and pursue the best of who you can be. You were created with everything you need to find the life you truly want. I have always felt a strong connection to a verse from the book of Romans. It has helped me in some of my darkest times; I believe in every word of it. I hope it keeps you well and in peace.

Romans 5:3-5[56]

And not only that, but we also boast in our sufferings, knowing that suffering produces endurance, and endurance produces character, and character produces hope, and hope does not disappoint us, because God's love has been poured into our hearts through the Holy Spirit that has been given to us.

Remember Churchill's words: "Never, never, never give up."

56 Holy Bible, New International Version®, NIV® Copyright © 1973, 1978, 1984, 2011 by Biblica, Inc.®

ABOUT THE AUTHOR

Former Air Force Major, CEO Bob Taylor

In *From Service to Success* Bob Taylor is sharing his real-life experience, from serving in combat as a B-52 navigator and then as a radar navigator, to one of his most challenging life transitions: an Air Force career he loved to family man with a successful career.

Bob Taylor attained a mechanical engineering degree from Michigan State University in 1986 then joined the Air Force in 1987. Bob married the love of his life, Sara, on the Fourth of July during navigator training. He finished that training program as a Distinguished Graduate. Shortly after, Bob was stationed at Griffiss Air Force Base, in New York. He then deployed to Diego Garcia, where he flew eleven combat missions during

Operation Desert Storm and received the Air Force's Air Medal. Shortly thereafter, Bob served as a KC-135 navigator and finally as an Air Force Academy Liaison Officer in the US Air Force Reserves.

Bob has dealt with the impact of his service for over 30 years, has worked within the VA health system for the last 10 years, and finally embarked on researching this book over the last six years. Bob has first-hand experience with the gaps in veteran care.

Since his transition from military service, Bob has concentrated on the medical device industry, where he has started five new companies and sold two. Today, Bob is the CEO, founder, and owner of Alliant Healthcare Products, Alliant Biotech, and Medisurge – the Alliant Family of Companies located in Grand Rapids, MI. Since 2002, his verified Service-Disabled Veteran-Owned Small Business has sold over $750 million in healthcare products to the VA and military hospitals all over the world.

Bob now lives on Torch Lake in northern Michigan

***

From Service to Success is the cornerstone of the Patriot Promise® Foundation, which Bob created to help drive down suicides among veterans and provide a clear path to a purpose-filled life after service. The foundation establishes non-profit ventures run 100% by veterans. The grand purpose is to offer veterans the ability to learn new skills in the workplace while also learning to enhance their lives. The Patriot Promise: Helping veterans find a new mission and new purpose and a new journey to a great life.

Learn more at: www.patriotpromise.org

CPSIA information can be obtained
at www.ICGtesting.com
Printed in the USA
JSHW020800101122
32883JS00002B/2